Acknowledgm

I want to thank eve
understanding, kindn pport they provided me with through this horrific chapter of my life.

To all my family members, friends and their friends, my dogs, even strangers at times, and some of my doctors, you have all contributed to my success of getting clean, staying clean, and bringing back some normalcy to my life.

Most, but not all, have been mentioned in my book at some point. For those who are not mentioned, I know who you are, and you are greatly appreciated and loved. As much as I would like to name you all individually, it would be a never-ending list of personal angels.

During my addiction and withdrawal, everyone who was aware of my situation always made every effort to do what they could to make me comfortable, even if it was the smallest of things, like letting me sit in the front seat of the car or serving me food. Even some of the minor things were the most difficult for me.

During this time, the people who shared my life had a knack for knowing when I was either down and depressed or in pain. They learned how to pick up my spirits or when just to let me be. That was not actually as easy as you would think, considering how erratic my personality had become.

Special thanks to my loved ones who had to live with me and endured all my shit day-in and day-out for all those years. Although they really didn't have a choice, they accepted it and dealt with it in their own ways. I know they all still have bad memories that can't be erased, forgotten, or forgiven, but most have all moved on from those dark days. I owe my life to every single one of you, and I will be forever indebted to you.

God bless you all!

Special Thanks

I want to give a special shout-out to three people that contributed greatly to getting my book published.

First, is my eldest son Brett. He provided his professional expertise in radio production along with his natural radio voice to narrate and produce the Audible version of this book. Having him do the narration was very special to me.

Second is his wife, Allyson. She provided her professional expertise in editing to give my book the final polish. She kept the book exactly the way I speak and the way I wanted to deliver it.

Third and finally is my wife, Chris. When I wrote this book and all the chapters, it was like putting a puzzle together to make it flow. She used her professional expertise to make this happen. She also designed the book cover which exemplifies the total chaos that surrounded my life and everyone around me during my addiction.

All three people had to endure reliving the darkest period of my life and accepted the challenge. I know for a fact, there were many times I would have to just stop and break away because of the bad memories. I'm sure it wasn't easy for any of them either, but I am truly appreciative of their commitment.

Table of Contents

Chapter 1: My Story

This is the story of my journey since suffering a back injury on January 11th, 2001, and how, within a year of my injury, I was completely addicted to narcotics without even realizing it, until it was too late.

Addiction comes in many forms. My addiction was with opioids prescribed to me as part of a "Pain Management" regimen following my injury.

I decided to write this book to share the last 20 years of my life. I hope that people who read this book will learn about the disease of addiction and seek help before it's too late.

In the beginning, I'll share a little about my life as it was before the injury and the many ways this injury turned my life and the lives of all those dear to me into a living hell over the next decade. This included my wife, children, extended family, and friends. Sometimes, my hell would fall at a complete stranger's feet at no fault of their own.

Pretty much everyone, at some time, has either known or knows someone suffering from some form of addiction, and probably most of you have known or know someone with opioid addiction.

I'll detail how my consumption of narcotics began and escalated through the years, all in the name of "Pain Management". How fast the quantity and potency of the prescribed narcotics increased, and the insanity of it all.

I will reveal how my addiction affected my relationships, sometimes nearly destroying them, and the mental and physical toll that addiction takes on others who share your life.

I will share my experiences with the struggles and determination that it takes for not only the addict to get clean but also how difficult it is for others around the addict. For me, the withdrawal process took over 2 years. I’ll share the step-by-step process that I used to get completely off the drugs.

I'll describe how the drugs changed my physical appearance and personality, not in a good way. I'll relate stories of some of my unexplained, explosive outbursts and actions, mostly without me feeling any guilt.

My loved ones will share their thoughts, feelings, and experiences with me during my addiction and my road to recovery. When they provided their accounts, it was very tough, at times, for me just to read them. Not that I disagreed with what they had to say, but the difficulty was reliving the reality of the harm I inflicted upon them.

I will describe the day I had an epiphany and decided to accept the challenge of wanting to be drug-free as well as all the thought and preparation, mentally and physically, it took for such a challenge.

I will share the numerous surgeries I've had to endure since being clean, without being afforded any narcotic pain meds for relief during and after these procedures.

I'll tell you about my daily challenges and even, sometimes, the fear my family had to be subjected to, never knowing what mindset I might be in when they would return home. My wife even said she didn't know if I'd be alive when she got home from work, considering the incoherent state I'd be in after my daily doses of narcotics.

Now, after 10 years of sobriety, I've gotten most of my life back together. Unfortunately, during my addiction, I had hurt many, if not all, of my loved ones to the point where my actions or words left them scarred. The hurt I cast upon them was always mental and never physical. They've mostly forgiven me, but the scars will last a lifetime.

There were definitely times of trials and tribulations for myself and everyone around me during my addiction and withdrawal period, which lasted, in total, about 12 years.

Most importantly, I want to make sure that everyone understands that, at the moment I decided to get clean, I had the resources, support, faith, and love to be successful. I was blessed that I didn't wait to get off the drugs until the point of losing everything.

My book has been written to share the before, during, and after-effects that narcotics have on a person who becomes addicted. Hopefully, some of my writings will enlighten and give hope to people who are addicted and to the loved ones around the addict that their situation can change.

This change isn't an easy one, but as a 10-year recovering addict, the fight was well worth it.

So many times, during my addiction, I could have given up, or my loved ones could have given up on me, but neither they nor I did. Trust me, at times, I just wanted to end everything and stop the madness.

As you read, I hope you will find a few of the tools that helped me get to this point of my life valuable. I am now a drug-free person who has received a second chance at living and rebuilding relationships with the possibility of helping others with their addiction.

Please enjoy and learn from my story. For those who are suffering, "DON'T EVER GIVE UP!" The downside of giving up will only bring sadness, depression, destruction, loneliness, and eventually, a shortened and miserable existence, leading to death.

Chapter 2: My Better Half

Until the infamous day of my injury, I was a very healthy 43-year-old man. I was employed, very active, happily married to Chris, who is English, and father to three young children. Brett was 16, Erica 13, and Bradley 7 years old. Chris is my second wife and the mother of Bradley. At that point, Chris and I had been married for 8 years. I'll share more about each of them later in the book as my journey continues.

First, I'll spend some time telling you all about Chris for many reasons, but primarily for being the catalyst behind my successful recovery.

I met Chris in March 1993 while she was visiting her childhood friend Tony, who had been transferred to the United States with his computer firm a few years earlier. The day I met her was a Friday, and I had been hanging out with some friends in Point Loma during the day.

At that time, I was living with my father, Keith, in the house that I grew up in, located in the San Carlos area of San Diego. I lived with my father because I had recently separated about 4 months earlier and was starting a divorce proceeding from my first wife.

After spending the afternoon with my friends, I decided to head back to my father's house, but not without stopping by a local bar to have a few beers. The bar's name was "Foggy's Notion" and was directly across the street from the San Diego Sports Arena. The Sports Arena was where everyone who grew up in San Diego went to see concerts, sporting events, the circus, roller derby, wrestling (real wrestling, haha), and everything else.

As I sat by myself at the bar at Foggy's watching some Basketball on the T.V., two girls and their male friend entered the bar. When they went to sit down, one of the girls sat next to me, and the other girl sat on the other side of her. The girl sitting next to me immediately introduced herself as Angela and starting to talk to me; she was a talker.

Angela introduced the other girl as Chris, who, at first, didn't say much to join in the conversation. The moment Chris did speak, I could tell she was British and had that funny accent.

As the night went on, the conversation between all of us never seemed to miss a beat. The guy they were with was eventually introduced as Tony.

When Tony and Angela decided to get up and do some dancing, that left Chris no option other than to talk to me one on one, and Boom, that's all it took. Chris and I talked for the rest of the night and even danced a bit ourselves. Being from two different countries, we were so different in every way that I found it so easy to talk to her.

As it turned out, Chris was leaving to go back to England that Sunday, so that gave me less than 2 days to get to know her better.

After much persuasion, I convinced Tony and Angela to let me give Chris a ride back to Tony's apartment. His apartment was very close to my father's house.

Chris and I got in my truck and left, arriving first to the apartment. I asked her if she could go out to dinner the next night before she left to go home to England. She said "Yes," but Tony wanted to go with us. He said he wanted to spend her last day in the States with her.

I'm sure he wanted to ensure Chris would be safe. I must say I was bummed out that Tony had to tag along.

Saturday evening came, and I went to pick up both Chris and Tony. We headed over to the Hotel Del on Coronado Island for some drinks, then to the Brigantine Restaurant for dinner. As it turned out, the evening was very enjoyable, even with the third wheel.

During dinner, I learned Chris was coming back to San Diego in July on a 6-month traveling visa. I was so pleased to hear that. Chris was the kind of girl I had never dated or hung out with before, and I really wanted to get to know her a lot more.

Sunday morning arrived, and it was time for Chris to go to the airport for a long journey home. Her direct flight was almost 14-hours from San Diego to London.

I went to pick her up at Tony's apartment. I was already feeling sad that I had only a little time to get to know her. When she answered the door, she greeted me with a friendly little hug and kiss, which picked up my spirits.

I bought her a bottle of Clos Du Bois Merlot to take with her. I then told her, "I would love to share it with you if you would allow me to come and see you in London."

Her face expressed excitement, but I knew what she was thinking, Yeah, right, he'll never make that journey; I just met him a few hours ago!

After Chris returned to England, we exchanged phone calls at least once a week. That was when long-distance calls abroad were still quite expensive. She made up for it by sending funny, cheerful greeting cards a couple of times a week. I always looked forward to checking the mailbox to see if another card had come.

About a month later, I made arrangements to go to England and see Chris. Traveling abroad was pretty easy for me. At the time, I worked at FedEx, and employees of FedEx had flying benefits. This benefit cost me only a few dollars for the 5,500-mile plane ride.

During my flight, I sat next to an older woman, and we started to chat. She asked me what was bringing me to England, and I went on to tell her about Chris and I meeting. She thought that was so nice and found it kind of romantic. She wished me luck and to have fun in her great country.

Upon arriving at Heathrow International airport bright and early the following morning and making my way through British customs, I met up again by chance with my elderly flying companion.

She asked if I had met up with my friend that I met in San Diego yet. I explained to her that I actually took an earlier flight than I had scheduled. This flight had arrived in London about an hour earlier than the flight I told Chris. She suggested that I go over to the Passenger Service Kiosk and have Chris paged over the intercom to meet up with me.

So off I went to do just that. I started to tell the Service Agent that I would like to have a person paged. The agent said, "no problem, what's her name?" At that moment, I was like a deer in headlights and somewhat embarrassed, realizing I didn't even know Chris's last name.

The agent didn't seem fazed, and she went to make the announcement for Chris over the intercom, saying, "Can Chris, who is meeting Greg from San Diego, please come down to the Passenger Service Kiosk to meet him?" As I waited at the kiosk, I wasn't only feeling embarrassed but also ashamed and disappointed for not knowing her last name.

As it turned out, Chris was already at the airport waiting for the scheduled flight that I told her. She was having a coffee right above me on the next level. Within a few minutes after the announcement, Chris met me at the kiosk. How nice it was to see her and hug her again.

We finally got to her car as we proceeded through the airport parking garage, and I tried to get into her driver's side door, completely forgetting the English drive on the WRONG side of the road. When I looked over at Chris, she was already laughing.

As we drove in her little Peugeot back to her flat (apartment) in the North Finchley area of London, I was in awe just taking it all in. It was like everything I had imagined. The design of the buildings and houses looked like they were straight out of the "Mary Poppins" movie.

Once we arrived at her flat, I was immediately introduced to her Collie mixed-breed puppy named Shadow, who went by the name Shaddy, we instantly bonded, and he quickly trained me to take him on walks!

Her flat was 2 stories, fairly large, and pretty impressive. It was an old Victorian building with a long deep narrow garden (backyard).

You would think at this point, all I would want to do was sleep, especially after the long flight with absolutely no sleep. But my anxiety was so high that I couldn't wait to go out and explore London, especially having a true Londoner as my personal tour guide.

As soon as I was unpacked, we headed out and drove to the local tube station (underground train) to head into the center of London and start taking in the sights.

During the day, we would duck into a pub to grab a pint, something we did a few times throughout the day. I loved the pubs; they were a blast.

Learning the ins and outs of riding the tube and jumping on and off the red double-decker buses to navigate through London was quite an experience. The public transportation in London is the best way to get through the city because the traffic is horrendous, and it will take you forever to get anywhere if you drive.

As the first day of sightseeing ended, we returned to her flat. On the way back, we decided to stop by Blockbuster Video to pick up a VHS video. You remember Blockbuster Video and the VHS, right?

After the long day, we just wanted to go back and relax and watch a movie. The movie we picked was "My Cousin Vinny," and we also grabbed a pint of Haagen-Dazs chocolate ice cream.

Once we settled on the couch and began to watch the movie, Chris pulled out the bottle of Merlot that I gave her to take back to England when she left San Diego. We sat there drinking the wine, eating ice cream, and watching the movie.

To this day, "My Cousin Vinny" has a special place in our hearts.

This trip to England was only for a weekend arriving Friday and leaving on Monday.

A few months later, in May, I decided to go back to England for another weekend trip. That meant that I traveled to England twice in less than 2 months for short weekend stays.

That equates to over 22,000 air miles, and I probably would have flown over again if Chris didn't already have plans to come back to the United States.

Chris came back in July, and I met her at the airport. She was a welcome sight for sore eyes, even though it had only been 2 months since we saw each other.

Back in 1993, you could go to the actual gate to meet your visitors. Wow, how things have changed since then.

I took her back to Tony's apartment, where she would be living for the next 6 months, and let her get settled in.

During the next 6 months, we would date and hang out, but we would still do our own thing. I was getting out of a failed marriage, and the last thing I wanted was to get into another steady relationship right away.

As the months went on, we started to do most things together. Chris was getting to really know Brett and Erica, my children from my previous marriage. Brett and Erica were 7 and 4 years old and became comfortable with Chris and enjoyed being around her. I think they could tell I was happy being with her.

Shortly after Chris arrived in July, Erica asked me, "When is your friend going home?" but it didn't take long for Erica's feelings to change and do a complete 180-degree turnaround. She loved hanging out with Chris and gave her the nickname "Kidda."

Chris's visa was ending in January of 1994, and she would be required to return to England. She wouldn't be allowed to return to the United States without waiting at least a year before being allowed to return on another Travel Visa. I didn't want to see her go, even if it were for only a year or so, and neither did Brett and Erica.

Everyone who came to know Chris soon felt the same way; they didn't want her to leave.

"Oh, she's so good for you."

"Oh, you guys are so good together."

I think everyone was more caring of her than me; just kidding!

After spending 4 or 5 months hanging out with Chris, I really got to know her. I enjoyed being with her; I could feel myself seriously starting to fall for her. Even though I tried to fight those feelings, I couldn't help myself.

There was never any drama with her. After these months, I knew she wasn't the type of girl who was out to try and change me or mold me into someone I wasn't.

In late November of 1993, after much serious thought and consideration, I decided to ask her to marry me. To my surprise and without any hesitation, she said "yes," and the wedding plans began.

Choosing a date for our wedding, Chris thought it would be nice if we married exactly a year from the date that we met on March 19th. I agreed, and we made wedding plans for March 19th, 1994, on the Bahia Belle on Mission Bay in San Diego. The Bahia Belle is a 2-story paddlewheel boat with a top deck.

The invites were sent out, and the guests from England and elsewhere made their travel plans.

Since her visa was expiring in January, 2 months before our planned wedding, she contacted the INS (Immigration and Naturalization Service) to seek an extension.

The INS informed her she couldn't get an extension and that she would have to leave the United States, return to England, and wait 6 months before she could apply for another visa.

Ouch, now what do we do? We'd made the reservations, paid deposits, and guests had made travel plans. Everyone from England and across the country had already bought their airfares, booked hotels, and sorted out all the other logistics that go along with a wedding.

After much discussion, I decided Chris and I should go to Las Vegas alone, not telling anyone, and just get married. Las Vegas offered a wedding package that included transportation to the courthouse to get the marriage license, transportation to the Candlelight Wedding Chapel for the ceremony, and then transport back to the Desert Inn Resort where we would be staying.

On the evening of December 17th, 1993, we left for Las Vegas and our secret wedding. I still remember the look on Chris's face once we came over the hill and saw the Las Vegas Strip's lights. She was like, "wow!"

The following day, Saturday, December 18th, as we prepared for our secret wedding, I became so nervous that I couldn't even tie my tie! I had to go downstairs to the concierge and have him assist me.

I also had this sick feeling in my stomach that I hadn't told anyone what Chris and I were up to.

After getting my tie sorted out, I decided to give my sister Vicki a call and let her know what was about to take place. It was before everyone had cell phones back then, so I had to go to a phone booth.

I made the call, and she was so excited for the two of us. I could also tell in her voice she was also a bit disappointed that we didn't let them know. She said they would have loved to be with us on this special day, but she said she understood.

We were picked up in a limousine from our hotel early in the afternoon. We were driven to the Clarke County Courthouse to apply for the marriage license. Chris was dressed in a cream knee-length dress - she looked beautiful - and I was in a suit.

Upon arriving at the courthouse, there was a line of other couples waiting to apply for their licenses. Some of the brides standing in line were in full-length white wedding gowns and long streaming veils. Kind of funny to see if you were there.

Once the marriage license was issued, the limo driver drove us over to the wedding chapel for the ceremony.

The minister who greeted us appeared to be a bit intoxicated and had already started his drinking for the day. We weren't sure he'd be able to stand through the vows!

The minister asked us where our witnesses were? Chris and I must have missed this memo. He suggested we go out to the Strip and ask some random strangers to be our witnesses.

Seeing a bride and groom out on the Las Vegas Strip looking for witnesses must have been quite a sight. It sounds strange, but it was, after all, Las Vegas! We found witnesses, and the ceremony proceeded; Chris and I were officially married.

Our marriage is a testament of time because neither the Candlelight Wedding Chapel nor the Desert Inn Resort are still in existence.

We still had our originally planned wedding on the Bahia Belle on March 19th, 1994. Again, nobody knew other than my sister and brother-in-law that we went to Las Vegas three months earlier and tied the knot, only to avoid the deportation requirement of her Travel Visa.

The March wedding was also very special for both Chris and me. Chris had all her family and friends there from the U.K., and I had all my family and friends there too. The big exception was my mother's absence, who had passed many years prior. My mother sure would have loved Chris, and it's a shame they never got to meet.

Once the boat left the dock the ceremony pretty much started. We completed our vows for the second time, and the party started, and it was quite the party.

We provided an open bar with only the best booze, music, and dinner. By the end of the night, both families and all our friends had become one big family. Everybody was talking to everybody, really making connections, and having a great time.

After roughly 7 years of marriage, I convinced Chris to apply to become a U.S. citizen. She completed her citizenship application at the beginning of 2000. Nearly 2 years later, she was notified to appear for an immigration interview, which I was required to attend with her. Within 2 months of the interview, Chris was granted her U.S. citizenship. America is lucky to have her as a citizen

Chapter 3: My Children

Let me briefly share a little information about my kids because I can't understate how much support all three of them provided me, not only during my addiction but every day since.

Brett graduated from San Diego State University in 2011. He went on to work for an online university, where he met his wife, Allyson. Brett and Allyson were married in October 2017 in the La Jolla area of San Diego. Brett has since switched careers and gone on to be a radio producer for the San Diego Padres, the San Diego State Aztecs Basketball and football teams, and KIIS FM-L.A. Currently, he is an Executive Producer for PodcastOne in Beverly Hills. He and Allyson relocated to Sierra Madre, a suburb of Los Angeles, and Allyson continues to work for an online University.

Erica graduated from Azusa Pacific in 2015 and works in Medical Administration. She was married to Jonatan in February 2019 at the Welk Resort in Escondido, a city about 25 miles north of San Diego. Jonatan also works in Medical Administration. They purchased a home with lots of land in Santee, CA, in November of 2019. They have three dogs, and their large lot is perfect for the dogs to run around and play on.

Bradley graduated from Sonoma State University in 2016 and is currently serving in the United States Air Force. He married Maddison (Maddie), his High School sweetheart, in October of 2020 at the Glider Port in La Jolla, just a bit south of Torrey Pines Golf Course. Their original plan was for a large wedding with 200 guests, but this had to be changed due to the COVID situation and restrictions, and it ended up being immediate family only. Brad deployed to the Middle East in January of 2020, returned safely in August of 2020, and is currently stationed in Charleston,

South Carolina. Brad and Maddie have a lovely apartment in Mt. Pleasant, about 30 minutes from his base. Maddie still works for the company she worked for in San Diego, but now she works remotely from Mt. Pleasant.

As you can tell, I have been truly blessed to have three great kids with college degrees and fantastic spouses. Chris and the kids are true blessings, and I can honestly say, if it hadn't been for them, I would have never survived the journey I'm about to tell you.

So many people contributed to and are responsible for my success in sobriety and my survival. Chris is the one who took the brunt of my pain, aggravation, hostility, and craziness, but the kids, Brett, Erica, and Brad, were next on the totem pole.

My sister and brother-in-law, Vicki and David, their daughters Amber and Ashley, and, of course, my father Keith were always there for support, love, and comfort.

Throughout the book, they'll be sharing individually the experiences they had to go through with me and my addiction. Everything they share will be put in the book exactly how they wrote it. I'll also share my feelings about each of them later on.

Chapter 4: My Loved Ones

I dedicate this chapter to my loved ones who had to live with me and experience all the pain and mental anguish I was going through, as well as the pain I subjected them to.

I asked my immediate family to write a short piece for me to be included in my book. They've written explaining their experiences and feelings toward me during the 10 years of my addiction.

This was the first time I had heard a lot of their comments. Obviously, they were too afraid to express their feelings at the time, fearing how I would react. I didn't have a very good track record when hearing something I disagreed with.

During my time of addiction, my personality changed significantly. I had become a person who could and would explosively react to pretty much anything at any time. Now that I have a clearer thought process, and I remember some of my explosive altercations with my family, I realize they only had good intentions for my health and wellbeing at the time, along with the health and wellbeing of everyone around me.

Some will share the love they had for me and, at other times, the disdain and sometimes downright hatred they had toward me for what I had become.

Often, the disdain and hatred they felt I brought upon myself for the way I acted, spoke to, and treated people. Unfortunately, I took my frustration over the never-ending pain that I was experiencing out on my loved ones.

For some strange reason, I thought my behavior and how I would treat people at times was acceptable and that they should understand.

Over time, their tolerance for my behavior wore thin, and some made decisions to limit their interactions with me. Limiting their interaction wasn't an option for Chris or Brad, who lived with me 24/7.

Chris and Brad's only escape from my persona was work for Chris and school for Brad. Trust me, neither one of them were in a hurry to come home. When they came home, I'm sure they were scared to some degree, not knowing what kind of mood I was going to be in.

That wasn't an environment that any wife or young child should have been subjected to. This, by no means, is to minimize the tension and fear my other loved ones had to experience.

Unlike Chris and Brad, the other family members could live their lives in some degree of normalcy because they could block me out of their thoughts if they weren't around me. However, they didn't completely abandon me because of the unconditional love and support they offered.

My whole family has been raised not to turn your back on family. These morals are deeply ingrained and have been demonstrated by each of them at one point or another. I can honestly say if it hadn't been for this quality that every member of my family showed, I wouldn't be alive today.

Even after 10 years of sobriety, I still sense that, at times, they have some doubts about my trustworthiness, integrity, and choices and decisions.

As the years go by, I feel like their doubts are slowly fading, and my previous relationships with each of them are improving and being rebuilt. The following few chapters include their stories precisely printed the way each one was written.

Chapter 5: A Letter from My Eldest Son, Brett

I remember my dad being Superman. I remember him flying through the air in Mission Bay as he backflipped off of a floating dock into the water below him. I remember his physical strength: lifting, carrying, and moving things with the least bit of effort. He could throw a baseball harder than anyone I knew. I remember his ability to read people and get the best out of them. Most importantly, my dad had this uncanny ability to sense when others needed help. He would always show up and save the day.

When I was a kid, my dad worked as a beer distributor, a mailman, and a FedEx courier. Like Superman, whatever the task entailed, he suited up and delivered. As I grew up, I realized that was a common theme in my dad's actions: he showed up, and he delivered. Whether it was coaching Little League games, helping with Boy Scout projects, or teaching me how to drive a car, he showed up, he delivered. He had an identity. My dad knew who he was to his family, his friends, and to the world. He knew what was needed of him, even when we didn't, and he always rose to the occasion. When he encountered an obstacle, he faced it and overcame it. He protected those who needed protecting and defended what he knew was right for him and for the ones he loved.

Then he broke his back and his tailbone, and Superman was brought to his knees by pain no one should endure.

I'll never forget the next decade, not because my father proved again how he could overcome any obstacle, but because he finally lost. A "doctor" prescribed him Vicodin, Oxycontin, Soma, and other medications I had never heard of before.

Medicine is supposed to be good for you, and we trusted those meds that ruined the next ten years of our lives.

As the medications increased, my father faded. Instead of taking off and backflipping into a pool, he would "take off" in a different way. We'd have my dad for an hour or two before he was drifting off, washing away into a place of oblivious comfort. He'd become mentally and socially absent but able to tolerate the pain. We didn't like this reaction, this "medical treatment," but it made the pain somewhat bearable for him. We didn't understand the dark place the meds would take him. His moods would swing between anger, frustration, and justifiable self-pity. He started breaking down the ones he cared about, seemingly without notice. Whether it was my stepmom, my sister, my brother, other family members, friends, or complete strangers, we all faced that darkness in one way or another.

We tried to act normal, carrying on with holidays, dinners, baseball, and softball games. We convinced ourselves life was still normal. We went on trips to take him out of his routine, hoping to find the person he was before the meds. But then the fights began. Whether it was at a family gathering, an amusement park, a restaurant, or a hotel room in Florida, he would get in our faces. He wouldn't back down. He became belligerent, eager to fight as if it helped him avoid fading away. My dad didn't care whom he hurt or who was watching, and my stepmother often had to physically stand between him and his new enemy.

Fights and altercations seemed more worth it to him, and, like the meds, he continued to dig deeper and deeper. At first, I thought he was addicted to the destruction. But then I realized it was the medications, how they seemed to put him in a bubble. And still, we continued trying to convince ourselves that it's just medicine. How can it be wrong?

The meds pushed us out. We feigned normalcy while my dad continued to fade. I never knew what was going to set him off. Happy moments became rare as he fell apart.

He and I started to see each other less and less. I think in avoiding him, I was avoiding a mixture of fear and sadness. Fear of how awful the situation had become. The overwhelming sadness of having to watch my Superman throw us away. I started college and tried to find other things to focus on. For years, I "wouldn't be able to make it" for dinners, for weekends, and for trips.

My fear and sadness manifested into pure resentment. For what he became. For his apathy. I didn't matter anymore; our family didn't matter anymore. When we did see each other, I told him how I really felt. I thought, If I fight, he'll know I care, and if he knows I care, he'll know I love him.

I'll admit now that I struggled to show compassion. I wanted to hurt him. I'd call him pathetic. I wanted to take my pain out on this man who was already at his lowest. I needed to pay him back for all that he did to me, to us. Just like I thought he was doing, I wanted to burn it all down, the good and the bad. I wanted to start over.

But still, I couldn't forget the person he once was, Superman. And my dad and I both realized that we were never going to give up on him.

Palm Springs, 2009, he told us for the last time that he was going to quit. And for the first time in almost eight years, I believed him. With a sad dread in his eyes, he seemed to finally recognize the damage that had been done and the journey he had ahead to salvage the broken pieces. I was cautious, but I finally saw that first glimmer of light so far down this dark tunnel. The dark tunnel we all had been traveling down with him. I realized that my dad needed to recover when he was ready to. It was going to be tough, for him, for all of us, but more than ever, he knew that we were all in it for the long haul. He hadn't lost any of us, and we were going to be there for him, whether he wanted it or not.

He went through hell to get off the meds. The loss of sleep, the constant sweats, the mood swings; it was clear that these drugs were fighting to stay a part of his life, just as we were. In a dark irony, these drugs reacted similarly to how I reacted as I felt my dad was "quitting" us. They fought viciously to remain.

Eventually, his smile came back. He began to enjoy things with a sober mindset, one not fogged by Somas, Oxycontin, and Vicodin. He became far less volatile. He started to help again: giving his family solid advice, donating his now clean blood to those who needed it, volunteering for church, and finally returning to the world he belonged in and could improve.

Deep down, I knew he always cared for us, but he started to express these feelings more often to his family and friends. His ability to read people and know what they truly needed, whether it was a hand, a hug, or just someone in their corner, was back. He wasn't backflipping or lifting things like he once did. He had a different strength to show now, a new strength I grew to respect, love, and admire more than what I once looked up to as a child, one that still makes me think of one name, Superman.

Dad, I thank God we have you back.

Brett is the oldest of my three children and has the biggest heart in the world. Even though Brett and I have never really discussed the effects of his mother and I divorcing when he was only 7 years old, considering his "heart of gold," I'm sure the divorce really took a toll on his childhood in many ways.

For a few years prior to the divorce, I was very involved in Brett's sports, most of the time being a coach. If I wasn't coaching him, I was in the stands being his number-one fan.

After the divorce, the ability to continue being a coach for his sports was taken away from me. I changed careers and went to work for FedEx and my new schedule impacted the time it took to be a dedicated coach. I tried to make it to most of his games and continued to cheer him on.

After my injury, I knew our relationship had withered over time. Everything he has written about me is true and I can't take any of it back. I knew in my heart he had these feelings of resentment toward me, but I never really wanted to accept them.

The visitation schedule for Brett and Erica was pretty much standard for most California divorces involving kids. I would have them every Thursday night and every other weekend along with switching major holidays every year.

For almost 11 years of following the visitation schedule and until Brett turned 18, there were only a couple of times that I was unable to fulfill this schedule.

As the years went on with my "Pain Management," I began to sink deeper into the darkness of my drug habit. Brett started to give excuses to opt out of some of the visitations, which irritated me, but I knew in my heart the real reason why.

As far as the annual vacations that Chris always insisted on, there may have been just one trip that Brett didn't go on, and that was just a conflict of schedules. Brett knew before these trips that they held the potential for me having a "meltdown" over something stupid, which would cause him embarrassment, fear, or pain, or the trifecta of all three, but he still went with us.

Even before my injury, I didn't consider myself "Father of the Year." A little story that Brett will never forget is when we went to San Diego Chargers football games.

A group of my friends all had season tickets for the Chargers, and we would gather in the same spot in the stadium parking lot hours before the start of the game. We would eat, drink, and have lots of laughs. Great times!

When it was time to enter the Stadium for the game, I would smuggle a few beers in, so I didn't have to pay the outrageous prices for the Stadium's stale, flat, and disgusting beer.

This is how the beer smuggling operation went. I would take my binoculars out of their case and hang them around my neck. I would put 4 beers into the empty binocular case, hang the case with the beers around Brett's neck and walk right past the security guards. Definitely not a good example for a father to set for his son, but Brett and I have laughed about this memory numerous times over the years.

When Brett was in high school, he was a member of the drama program. A few of the plays Brett performed in were *Snoopy* and *The Little Shop of Horrors,* along with others. Loving to perform, Brett and a few of the other drama members started an improv comedy show that they performed every other month.

When his performances were on the calendar, it gave me something to look forward to. I knew after each show I would be coming away with a big smile on my face from the laughter of the performances, especially the improv gigs. The performances were spontaneous and really bought out the member's individual talents...and Brett would always hit a home run!

There is one thing Brett said to me during my addiction, and I've never forgotten it because it brought me to a new low spot in our relationship at the time. He said, "Dad, when I talk to you on the phone, you always seem to be preoccupied, and I feel like you could care less about talking with me."

I took his comment and gave it some serious thought, only to realize he was right. It wasn't that I could care less about talking to him; it was the fact that when we were talking, I wasn't really paying attention to what he was saying.

From that point on, every time we speak, I make every effort to give him my undivided attention and listen to every word he has to say.

That one statement made me aspire to be a better person because I knew Brett wasn't the only person I would blow off and not listen to when talking on the phone.

Now that I live in Florida, I get out to San Diego to see everyone at least every three months. Seeing the kids and their spouses is a priority and always one of the first things to get on the schedule, and for as many times as possible. The quality time spent during these visits is fantastic and always enjoyable, and the visits are only getting better.

I feel like our relationship is the best it has ever been for both of us. Words cannot express how grateful I am that you didn't give up on me and have allowed me to always be in your life. I'm genuinely thankful that you found such a great wife as Allyson to share your life with.

Love you, Brett and Allyson!

Chapter 6: My FedEx Courier Position

First, let me explain my position at FedEx. I was a courier and absolutely loved my job. My schedule consisted of working Monday through Thursday.

I would start my workday around 6:00 am, and the day would end anywhere from 6:00 pm to 7:30 pm.

Shortly after arriving at work, I would conduct a vehicle inspection on the van, truck, or Grumman, whichever would be required to make a run to the airport to pick up the first overnight freight that needed to be delivered to the recipient before 8:00 am.

After completing the first overnight deliveries and returning to the FedEx Station, I would go to another vehicle that I would be using for the route that I would be on for the day.

I was called a "Floating Courier," and I considered it to be the best position at FedEx. Some couriers worked 5 days a week and others only 4 days a week. Those who worked 5 days a week worked an 8 to 5 Monday through Friday schedule. The ones who worked 4 days a week had the same schedule as I had - 6:00 am till whenever that day's outbound freight was off to the airport, generally around 7:00 pm.

Floating courier meant I would cover a particular courier's day off, a courier who had a 4-day workweek. So, every Monday, I would be running the same route, every Tuesday running the same route, and the same for Wednesday and Thursday.

Let me tell you a little something about the routes I had. On Monday, my route would start in Jamul and end up in Jacumba. This route didn't have a lot of deliveries (generally between 35 to

45 stops), but it had a lot of driving, sometimes over three hundred miles for the day. This route wasn't very physically demanding but could be mentally challenging.

This was a very rural route in the mountains of San Diego County, and most of the delivery recipients lived well off the beaten path away from anyone else.

First, I would find their mailbox, located on whatever the closest paved road might be. Then I would have to decide which dirt road I would proceed on. Sometimes, I chose correctly; other times, I didn't.

The recipient's home could be several miles down this dirt road. While driving down the dirt road, I wouldn't see any houses or structures and sometimes wondered if I'd made the wrong choice.

I would look for electrical power lines, knowing they supplied power to something. Once I located the house or structure, I would go to the door and try to get an answer.

If no one was there, and if the package was allowed to be left (without a signature), I always wanted to ensure I was at the correct location. Many of the homes located out in the middle of nowhere don't have house numbers.

I would have to look for something with an address on it. Most of the time, that meant looking through their trash for something with an address on it, such as a piece of junk mail.

Once I was sure I was at the right place and left the package, I would never forget how to get there.

This route ran along Highway 94 along the U.S./Mexican border, and I would frequently see illegal immigrant activities along with several Border Patrol checkpoints.

I have a funny story about something that happened to me on that route during the Christmas season. That's when the package volume increased significantly, and FedEx would have to rent additional vehicles to get the increased volume delivered.

On this particular day, I was in a yellow Hertz high cube truck. I had to go to a house with a backyard property line that backed onto the U.S./Mexican border.

After driving miles down this rolling black asphalt road and then onto the dirt road that led to the house, I was met by the homeowner who was anxiously waiting for his package. We had a short but friendly conversation about him being a retired Border Patrol officer.

As I headed back down his dirt road and got back onto the asphalt road, I came over one of the little hills and was met by two Border Patrol agents. They had their weapons pulled and pointed at me. They instructed me to get out of the vehicle with my hands above my head.

Once I was out of the vehicle, they immediately recognized my FedEx uniform but still weren't convinced I was employed with FedEx. They both approached me, still armed, but guns lowered a bit and asked me to open the roller door on the Hertz rental truck.

I walked toward the back and slowly opened the roll-up door as the agents stood there prepared, not knowing what they might find.

At this point of my route, it was near the end of my day, and I had only a few packages left to be delivered.

Once the agents were satisfied that I was who I said I was, we all had a little laugh. They explained that these types of rental vehicles are commonly used to smuggle drugs and illegal immigrants into the United States.

As I mentioned earlier, this route might take up to 300 miles of driving, and, often, I would be driving on dirt roads for 150 miles of that. There were only 3 or 4 couriers at FedEx who knew how to run this route

This was also at a time when cell phones were just becoming available. Even if you had a cell phone, there was no signal/reception due to the mountainous terrain. So that limited trying to call the recipient for directions to their home.

I would be in the San Diego State University area for my Tuesday route. This route had houses, apartment buildings, businesses, and parts of the college. It was also a busy route with lots of deliveries and pickups. This area had a high density, and parking was a challenge.

Chris (my wife) would meet me sometimes for lunch on this route because she worked not too far away.

This route was pretty much uneventful other than me hustling and running most of the day. As it turned out, the Tuesday route would be the last one I was ever on for FedEx because of my injury.

Wednesday was an interesting route that consisted of the "Mile of Cars" area of National City. This area was 95% car dealerships and businesses and required driving the Grumman's largest delivery vehicle in the FedEx fleet.

The Grumman would be completely filled with parcel packages, car parts, and FedEx letters and envelopes, several hundred of them. The thing about this route was that most of those deliveries would be required to be delivered by 10:30 am, FedEx's Priority Service.

My deliveries were generally finished by noon, allowing me to take a long lunch of 2 hours. Quite often, I would eat my lunch and get in the back of the Grumman to take a nap before I started the pickup cycle of my day.

Since this route was made up almost entirely of businesses on a typical day, I could have up to over 120 stops for delivery and pickup.

When I first began doing this route, I was preparing my packages in the back of my truck at the FedEx station before heading out to start the deliveries. I began to catch the smell of pot (marijuana) in the back of the truck where the packages were being put into delivery order. The smell was becoming stronger and more pungent, and I was thinking, "*Man, somebody is shipping a shitload of pot!*"

I decided to inform my manager of the smell, and when he came over, he just started to laugh uncontrollably. He then told me that the smell was coming from packages going to be delivered to the DEA (Drug Enforcement Agency) Laboratory for testing.

When the DEA confiscates drugs from illegal activities, the drugs are sent off to the DEA Lab to test potency and quantity.

I soon learned to make the DEA Lab stop the last stop of my "Priority" deliveries. The DEA protocol for receiving evidence deliveries is for one dedicated individual to be responsible for receiving these types of deliveries.

This individual would inspect every package separately to ensure the box hadn't been tampered with. This delivery might be in 10 separate packages or more, and it always took some time to verify that they hadn't been tampered with. The receiving person would never sign for the delivery until the inspection process was completed. The person's name would have to be entered into the tracker by 10:30am in order to have proof of delivery before the commitment time.

The area this route covered was very small and compact, allowing me to deliver up to 30 stops in an hour and maybe 15 to 20 pickups an hour. Pickups always took a longer time to complete because of the paperwork. Sometimes, the shipments weren't always ready to be shipped, even though the shipper would say they were prepared at a particular time.

My Thursday route, which was a rural route in the mountains with lots of driving and maybe 35 to 45 deliveries and pickups, started in the town of Alpine and ended up at the U.S. Air Force Radar Station on the top of Mount Laguna. The highlight of this route was the view to the east overlooking the deserts of Southern California, including El Centro and Borrego Springs. What a beautiful view it was.

One of the time-consuming stops would be to pick up fake ammunition that would be used in the movie/television industry. Boy, did I hate having to go out to that place!

Sometimes I would have to go out there to make a delivery and then go out there again for a pickup. Going out there twice would take up to 1 ½ to 2 hours alone—a real time-eater.

As I mentioned earlier, my work schedule at FedEx consisted roughly of 12-hour days Monday through Thursday, starting around 6:00 am to after 6:00 pm. It's amazing how fast a 12-hour workday goes by when you're continuously moving. Also, having a 4-day work week allowed me to have three-day weekends with Friday, Saturday, and Sunday off every week. That was so nice!

With this schedule, I would start my work week with a mild delivery and pickup day but lots of driving. Not much sleep was required the night before. I would have to hustle on Tuesday and Wednesdays and then have another mild delivery day on Thursdays, but again with lots of driving. God, I wish I were still doing this for a living, but, unfortunately, that wasn't in the cards.

Chapter 7: My Injury

So now, with a better understanding of my job, let me explain how my injury occurred on January 11th, 2001, in Descanso, California, while I was working for FedEx.

This is where my nearly 10 years of drug addiction - in the name of "pain management" - and treatment plan begins.

I was on my Thursday route from Alpine to Mount Laguna when I suffered my career-ending injury during a bizarre snowstorm in Descanso.

It was a cold, stormy day with blizzard conditions (believe it or not, considering San Diego's climate), and the snow had started to really drop fast.

I made a delivery that required driving up a long steep, asphalt driveway. The trip up the driveway was successful, but when it came time to return down the driveway, the weather conditions had severely worsened, and the black asphalt was frozen and iced. To make matters worse, the homeowner had parked his new Range Rover at the bottom of the driveway in anticipation of the bad weather.

I knew if I decided to drive back down the driveway, I would most likely be unable to control the FedEx vehicle, and it would start sliding uncontrollably and most likely take out the parked new Range Rover.

After consulting with FedEx dispatch, the decision was made to send out another vehicle and transfer all the freight into a new vehicle, leaving the first vehicle behind until the weather improved and the first vehicle could safely be retrieved.

The freight had to be loaded onto a hand truck/dolly and wheeled down the frozen driveway to transfer the freight from the stranded vehicle to the new vehicle.

I successfully made the trip down the driveway twice, but unfortunately, the hand truck went to slip on the third trip, and then I slipped and fell onto my butt.

With the freezing weather, I didn't feel anything except for the jarring hit my buttocks and spine took from the frozen ground. As the day continued, I started feeling pain and discomfort, thinking I possibly bruised my tailbone.

Once the freight was transferred into the replacement van, I became the passenger and let my coworker drive. Within minutes of going down the curvy iced road, the van skidded off the road and into a shallow ditch. My coworker and I were able to free the van from the ditch and continue making the remaining deliveries.

Since my injury occurred on a Thursday, I had the next three days off. I thought I would have the long weekend to feel better and improve. When Monday came around, my condition hadn't improved, but I was able to work with much pain and discomfort.

When Tuesday came, I went to work as usual and did my deliveries, still with the pain and discomfort as the day before. I was hoping to just make it through the day.

As I was making my pickups late in the afternoon, all of a sudden, my legs didn't want to work correctly, and I became really concerned about what was happening with them.

I notified FedEx of my situation, and they asked if I was able to drive back to the station or if I needed someone to come and get me. I was able to drive back myself, and upon my return to the station, I was told by management that I needed to go for some medical attention.

Since it was late in the evening, I said I would go to the doctor's first thing in the morning. That was unless my condition got so severe, then I would go immediately to the Emergency Room at the hospital. I made it through the night without worsening and went to the doctor bright and early the next day.

Chapter 8: FedEx Mandated Treatment

When you have a work-related injury at FedEx, you're required to seek treatment from a physician contracted with the company. Unfortunately, with these "company contracted physicians," I believe their primary goal is to minimize the injury when possible and get you back to work ASAP, which means going without the necessary testing to identify the injury and the source of the pain most of the time.

Taking these shortcuts minimizes the expense for treatment and doesn't get the patient the care required to make a complete recovery; it just puts the patient in a position for another injury or worsens the current injury.

I will refer to all of my doctors using fictitious names to protect myself and them from any legal ramifications.

The first physician I saw was the company doctor named "Dr. Dumb-Dumb." At first, he seemed genuinely concerned and interested in getting my injury diagnosed and starting a treatment plan. Dr. Dumb-Dumb started with what's known as a "Conservative Treatment Plan," which consisted of X-Rays, anti-inflammatories, and some basic pain medication.

After a month or so of the conservative treatment plan with NO improvement and my condition worsening, Dr. Dumb-Dumb suggested another approach. He prescribed a series of three epidural injections.

These injections were performed by "Dr. Butthead" and were executed at various surgery centers throughout San Diego.

After the second injection, I developed the worst headache of my life and conveyed this to Dr. Butthead. His response was that these headaches were common and would go away in a short time. He instructed me to increase the pain medication until the headache went away. Well, the headache didn't go away and wouldn't go away no matter what I tried to do.

I completed the series of three injections over 7 days, and still NO improvement for my back pain, and the raging headache continued with no relief and no concern from the doctor. Dr. Butthead's only comment was, "Give the epidurals some time to work."

After a couple more weeks, Dr. Dumb-Dumb told me that sometimes, it takes a few series of epidural injections to alleviate the pain and suggested I get another batch of three epidurals from Dr. Butthead.

I agreed to another series, but I complained relentlessly about my constant, debilitating headache to the doctors. However, they weren't concerned by this in the slightest.

After starting the second round of injections, I began to find it strange that every appointment with Dr. Butthead would be scheduled at a different surgery center location. I questioned Dr. Butthead about this and why he couldn't do the injection at the exact location each time. His explanation was, "It has to do with the surgical center's schedule, and I can't do anything about it." It sounded reasonable to me at the time, and I accepted his explanation.

It wasn't until arriving early one day at the parking garage for an appointment that my father and I saw Dr. Butthead arrive and park his car. We watched in amazement as he unloaded the trunk of his car with all sorts of supplies and thought this was very strange.

After completing the whole second round of injections and still not showing any signs of improvement and experiencing the worst headache, I decided it was time to switch doctors and get a second opinion for my treatment and care.

After a certain amount of time, a "Workmen's Compensation" patient can opt-out of the treatment they're receiving from the dictated insurance doctor. The patient can seek treatment from a doctor of their choice. Upon learning this, I started to review some new options and spoke to a few other people who had some similar experience in dealing with Workmen's Compensation.

I spoke with a coworker who had been involved in a horrific FedEx big-rig accident where he nearly lost his life. I shared my disappointment with him about how my treatment wasn't progressing well and the lack of improvement. He suggested I go to a doctor who treated him after his crash.

He also suggested that I get legal representation specializing in workplace injuries to protect myself, my right to proper medical care and treatment, and my future livelihood.

Getting concerned that I may never get rid of this headache and back pain, I decided to go with the doctor who treated him. The doctor's name was Dr. Steven, and I made an appointment for the first opening he had. My appointment was scheduled within a couple of days.

During my appointment, I learned Dr. Steven had some experience and knowledge about the cause of my headaches. He suggested that I see an anesthesiologist.

My immediate thought was I'd been seeing an anesthesiologist (Dr. Butthead) for nearly 2 months, and his treatment had done absolutely nothing to treat my back pain or the headaches.

Dr. Steven assured me the anesthesiologist he was referring to had plenty of experience with patients experiencing these types of headaches. As it turned out, my headaches were caused by a "spinal leak." Just these words gave me some hope that at least he knew the cause, and I could get relief from the headaches.

From that moment on, Dr. Dumb-Dumb and Dr. Butthead were in my rearview mirror and were never to be seen by me again.

I made an appointment with the new anesthesiologist. Within moments of meeting with the new anesthesiologist, he immediately diagnosed the cause and knew how to eliminate my "spinal leak" headache. The doctor explained to me that an "epidural blood-patch" procedure would rid me of my headaches, and he scheduled the procedure ASAP.

"An epidural blood patch is a surgical procedure that uses autologous (same individual) blood to close one or many holes in the dura mater of the spinal cord, usually as a result of a previous lumbar puncture. The procedure can be used to relieve post-dural puncture headaches caused by a lumbar puncture (epidural injection). A small amount of blood is injected into the epidural space near the site of the original puncture, and the resulting blood clot then "patches" the meningeal leak."

My 2-month-long extreme headache was caused when Dr. Butthead performed the second injection in the initial series of injections.

Apparently, when Dr. Butthead was locating where to place the epidural injection into the spine, he missed his target and had to try again. The missed attempt caused a puncture in my spinal dura mater (spinal cord casing), from which the spinal fluid leaked, causing a severe headache.

"This type of spinal leak causes the spine to contract and cause "intracranial hypotension." Other symptoms of spinal leaks can be, nausea, vomiting, neck pain and stiffness, hearing problems, imbalance, and sensitivity to light."

Immediately after my blood patch was performed, my headache was gone for good. I couldn't believe how long I had suffered because of Dr. Butthead's negligence and how quickly the headache went away with the simple blood patch.

I actually cried in the car with Chris after getting the blood patch procedure because I no longer suffered from the debilitating headache. I couldn't believe I had suffered for so long when there was a such an easy remedy.

Dr. Butthead could have performed the blood-patch procedure, but to do so, he would have had to admit to making the puncture in the first place when performing the epidural and accept fault. Plus, he would be held financially liable to correct it without reimbursement from the insurance company.

Thinking it was strange that Dr. Butthead wouldn't acknowledge his error and remembering how he had to provide all his own supplies for his cases, I decided to do some research on the good old Dr. Butthead.

Much to my surprise, I found that Dr. Butthead had had his medical license and hospital privileges suspended or revoked more than once.

I also found out why he had to provide his own medical supplies for all the procedures he performed. It was because he would use the surgical center supplies and not pay for them. The facilities stopped him from using their inventory. Kind of like dining and dashing!

Believe it or not, Dr. Butthead is still practicing medicine today!

I cannot emphasize enough how important it is to conduct your own due diligence and research your doctor's history, qualifications, and license status if you have a serious illness or injury. Do your research to find answers to the following questions:

Are they in good standing with your State's medical board?

Have they ever been reprimanded?

Have they ever had their license revoked or suspended?

Unfortunately for me, I didn't do my "due diligence," and I ultimately paid the price for it. Not only did I suffer longer than needed with the headache, but the original conservative treatment plan with Dr. Dumb-Dumb turned out to be more conservative and not aggressive enough.

When Dr. Steven became my attending physician, treatment became more aggressive, efficient, and attentive. Dr. Steven immediately got me scheduled with an MRI and other required testing to obtain a thorough diagnosis.

After the MRI was completed and reviewed by the neurosurgeon, it was determined that several of my spinal discs and vertebrae were damaged. The bulging of the discs was pinching the nerves, causing all the pain I was experiencing.

The problem for me was the fact that I had numerous levels of my spine that were damaged and needed attention. Prioritizing which level of the spine to address first to give me some relief was the primary goal.

In the meantime, FedEx's lawyers decided to take me to task. Before they would approve any kind of surgery or treatment, I would have to be subjected to many additional procedures such as myelogram, discogram, and electromyography.

The **discogram** is very barbaric. The anesthesiologist inserts a needle through the spine and into the disc. After the needle has been placed into the disc, pressure is applied by inserting a sterile liquid through the needle, causing pressure on the disc. If the disc is damaged, the patient will immediately be in excruciating pain to the point of tears. By documenting the severity of the pain, it is determined how damaged the disc is.

"The **electromyography** is where small needles are inserted through the skin on your thighs and into the muscle then given an electric shock to detect any neuromuscular abnormalities."

Not much fun getting poked with needles and waiting to get shocked.

After completing all of the required testing, it was determined I needed a "spinal fusion." Not a single-level fusion, but a 2-level fusion from L2-L4.

At the time, a 2-level fusion didn't have a high success rate, but for the extremely damaged condition my spine was in, it was my only option.

My First Surgery

My spinal fusion surgery was scheduled for September 12th, 2001, at Mercy Hospital in San Diego. The surgery was estimated to take around 8 hours to perform, and I would stay in the hospital for about 7 days to recover.

On the morning of September 11th, while I was mentally trying to prepare for my surgery the following morning, the United States experienced the 911 Terror Attacks. Like everyone else, I didn't know if America was at war or what was going on. After much talk with the surgeons and hospital, it was decided to proceed with the scheduled surgery as planned.

A lot was going on in my mind. Kind of scary knowing I'd be stuck in a hospital with no mobility if the attacks were the beginning of a war.

On Tuesday morning, September 12th, I was required to be at the hospital by 5:00 am. Upon my arrival, I was registered and prepped for surgery.

This was the hardest time for me, waiting to be carted off to the OR (operating room). When I was finally carted off, I couldn't help wondering if I would make it through an 8-hour surgery and if this would be the last time I was going to see my wife and family. I think everyone who goes through surgery has the same thoughts.

As I was wheeled into the OR, the surgery assistants were preparing all the surgical tools that were needed while rocking out to the booming music of Led Zeppelin. The music was actually quite comforting.

Before I knew it, I was under sedation, and the surgery was on. When the sedation cocktail was inserted into my IV, they asked me to count backward from 100, but I didn't even get to 95 before I was out! The last feeling I had before going under was the coolness of the sedation going up my arm.

Dr. Arthur performed my first spinal surgery, and it took roughly 8 ½ hours to complete. I made it through without any complications, and the professionals considered it a real success.

The procedure included the removal of what was left of my 2 discs between levels L2 and L4, and the insertion of cadaver bone along with titanium hardware rods and bolts.

In 2001, this type of surgery required cutting through my muscle mass and nerves, with an approximately 8-inch incision. The surgical tools used during these surgeries were still pretty brutal. These tools included power drills, saws, even a hammer, and a chisel. I'm sure they all have proper medical names, but they're the same tools found around the house.

The recovery time for this surgery was estimated to take almost 18 months for me to get as good as I was going to get.

After waking up in the recovery room and then returning to my hospital room, I had never experienced the amount of pain I had before, and that's with all the pain medication I already had in me.

The good old Morphine drip was the best relief option, but you can only push that button so often as it's a measured and timed dose. You can press the button as many times as you want, but if it's not time for the scheduled dose, there is NO drug available.

The physical therapist came in the next day after surgery to get me up and get my body moving again. On the first day with the therapist, I had to walk the hospital halls with my I.V. pole in tow.

The next day, the therapist had me go to the staircase and climb a flight of stairs. The I.V. pole became my best friend and provided the pain juice that allowed me to do these little tasks. After I completed my daily physical therapy, I was utterly exhausted.

The hospital room that I was in for the next week was on a higher floor and had a fantastic view to the west toward the bay and the Pacific Ocean.

For the first few days, I had a roommate who was dealing with kidney stones and the pain associated with that. After he was discharged, I had the room to myself, which was nice. I didn't have to worry about watching T.V. or how loud it was. I also didn't have to worry about the strange noises I would make due to the pain. There was a lot of moaning and groaning!

When I was finally discharged from the hospital and returned home, the pain was so severe that a "pain management regimen" was initiated.

Chapter 9: The Ups and Downs of Physical Therapy

The first pain medicine that was prescribed for my pain was Vicodin. With any kind of movement, the pain would be almost unbearable. For example, just wanting to roll onto my other side while lying down was probably the hardest thing I had to do. It was something I had to do, and I knew what the price would be for doing it: pain, pain, and more pain.

One side effect that I've experienced after every surgery is the feeling of being nauseated nonstop. It appears to be caused by the hours of anesthesia and the sedation cocktail used (I call it poison). This sickening feeling was no fun when it was added to the extreme pain that I was already experiencing. Enough is enough!

I was prescribed a medication called Ondansetron which is given to cancer patients to help reduce the feeling of nausea when receiving chemotherapy. It didn't really help me. The thing that helped me the most for the nausea was a product called "Cola Syrup," which can be purchased over the counter. It's the Cola syrup used in soda fountains like those used in a fast-food restaurant such as McDonald's or Burger King. The syrup is heavy and thick and definitely provided relief for my nausea.

My first big outing was my sister-in-law's wedding just 10 days after surgery. It wasn't much fun for me, considering the pain, but at least I was there to share the big event with her. The Hawaiian-themed wedding was held in their backyard and had a large number of guests in attendance. They even had a pig roasting in a firepit, which was a first for me! That's where I found out that a pig's testicles were an appetizer - not for me, thank you.

A concern that I had was that I didn't want to be the center of attention and wanted to keep the focus on the bride and groom. I was able to get situated and seated before most of the guests arrived, so my condition was pretty much under the radar for the ceremony. The wedding was a success, and everyone seemed to have a have a great time celebrating, including myself.

As it turned out, all I needed was a little Vicodin and a few beers to tolerate my pain. Since I was new to taking Vicodin, I didn't know then that narcotics and alcohol are a dangerous mixture and can cause accidental death by overdose.

I was required to wear a shell brace around my back and chest to limit my mobility, so I wouldn't damage any of the work that was done during the surgery. I soon learned how to protect myself from being vulnerable to incidents. This meant I looked and made sure of every step I took so I wouldn't trip or fall. I also learned how to position myself when I was out and about to minimize the risk of getting bumped into.

A few months after the first surgery, I decided to go and watch my son Brad's soccer game. As I stood on the sideline away from absolutely everyone, one of the players from the other team chased a ball that went out of bounds and ran straight into me. I might as well have been hit by a dump truck for the amount of pain this caused. That was the end of my outing for the day, and I had to immediately return home to recover.

About a month after surgery, I started a physical therapy (PT) program. This program consisted of riding a stationary bike, massage, heat, ice, and a TIMs stimulating unit. I was instructed to go three days a week for therapy for the foreseeable future.

Once I arrived at the PT Facility and got checked in at the front desk, the receptionist let the therapist know I was there. The therapist would get me started on the stationary bike, and I would ride for 15 minutes. After my bike ride, the therapist would continue with the other rehab therapies.

One day, I went to PT, as usual, checked in, and started riding the bike. After several minutes of riding, the bike's seat post either broke or wasn't totally in a locked position. This caused the seat, with me on it, to drop about 15 inches and come to an abrupt stop. At that point, I thought I was going to die from the pain this sudden fall caused. I was also really scared that this fall may have damaged the work that was performed during my surgery.

A call was made to my wife to inform her of what had happened and ask her to come and pick me up.

As soon as I got back home, I called Dr. Steven and was able to talk to him. He instructed me to get to his office as quickly as possible for an examination. Once Chris and I got to his office, we talked about what had happened, and he ordered a series of X-rays.

I went to the radiologist and had the X-rays completed and directly returned to Dr. Steven's office so he and I could review them. When he looked at the film, he discovered I had suffered a broken/dislocated coccyx (tailbone) from the fall. The pain I was experiencing was like having a sharp object stabbing you in the ass and tailbone. Ouch!

Dr. Steven was confident he could get this fixed right then and there. He described how it had to be done and that had me frightened. He started by saying he would insert his finger up my rectum, locate the coccyx, and pull on it to adjust it back into the correct position.

He insisted my wife be in the room at the time of the adjustment. I think it was so she could share in my trauma. Just kidding; I think it was for his protection too.

After the bike accident, I never returned to that PT facility again.

A couple of months after the coccyx adjustment, I was able to return to therapy at a new PT facility. It also meant that I would have to start at ground zero again regarding the therapy rehabilitation. That's when Dr. Steven really went to bat for me.

Dr. Steven insisted that FedEx, their lawyers, and their insurance agree to send me to Frog's Fitness Center for aqua therapy for the remainder of my PT, lasting almost 6 months.

The therapy at Frog's was much more professional and very intense. The therapist was always there upon my arrival to make sure I was physically prepared.

My routine would start by riding a stationary bike for 15 minutes after the therapist inspected it to ensure it was in proper working condition. That was never done at the previous PT facility. Then I would do a circuit of weight machines lasting around 20-25 minutes, starting with minimal weight and minimal movement and steadily increasing both over time.

Once I completed the indoor routine of bike riding and weights, I would proceed to the outdoor pool. The pool exercises were the most challenging and most demanding part of therapy.

I would put on floating ankle wraps along with a floating vest and get into the pool. The floaties would immediately want to pull my legs out from underneath me and flip me over. The purpose of these floating devices was to make me fight this urge and build up my core muscles.

I'm sure it was pretty comical at the beginning for anyone watching me flopping around in the water like a fish that had been hooked and was trying to get released. It took some time and a lot of sweat to master this. It soon became easier and easier, but then the therapist would introduce new maneuvers and exercises that demanded even more strength and determination to complete. I bet you didn't think you could sweat in a pool, but I was proof that you can.

After returning home from a PT session, I would be totally worn out and in a lot of pain. When I was in the water, my body joints decompressed, allowing me to have more movement and flexibility, but the pressure would return to joints with more intensity when I exited the pool.

After a few months of aqua therapy, I must say I was in the best shape of my life. I was pleased and proud of myself, but it took a lot of hard work and a lot of pain to get to that point.

As my treatment got more intense and the costs escalated rapidly, FedEx and their attorneys were trying to find some kind of mitigating factor to minimize their liability. They hired a private investigator (PI) to follow and videotape me, trying to catch me doing something I shouldn't be able to do, considering my injury.

The PI would follow me to Frog's Fitness Center and try to gain entrance to observe me doing my indoor bike and weight routine, but he was denied entry because he wasn't a club member. He still watched me through the fence when I was in the pool doing my PT thing.

On one occasion, the PI thought he had caught me in the act. Unfortunately for him, he was actually recording a friend of mine playing basketball in front of my house.

His declaration was "it was Greg shooting the basketball" when anyone could clearly see it wasn't me. Not even close to looking like me. Eventually, the PI had to admit he was wrong.

Another time, the PI sneaked around to the back of my house beyond my property in an open area. He was again hoping to catch me doing something, but who knows what?

While he was spying on me in my backyard, I had to make a trip to the store. When he realized I was leaving, he ran back to his truck to try and catch up with me. He had no idea I knew he was watching me.

Since I was just going to the grocery store, I allowed him to catch up to me. He didn't know where I was going. He stayed pretty close behind me in the right lane as I was driving in the left lane. At the very last moment, I pulled into the turn lane to enter the shopping center.

My decision to turn was too late for him, and he couldn't change lanes in time, so he had to continue to go straight. I parked and watched him make the first turn he could and drive through the parking lot looking for me. I have to say; I got a good laugh watching him scramble.

The PI had no success and struck out twice in the attempts that I witnessed. His expense was a complete waste of money for the insurance company. I learned over time that the insurance company would rather spend 10 times the amount of money to try and minimize their liability than to provide the proper care and treatment needed to recover from an injury.

Chapter 10: Life After FedEx

Since my first surgery in 2001 severely restricted my ability and hopes to return to FedEx in my normal capacity, I had some life-altering decisions to make.

What if I didn't return to FedEx? What would I do for work? My options were limited because my entire working career had been a very physical one. Now those strengths were no longer with me or had seriously been diminished.

Now I was basically a stay-at-home dad, spending quality time with the kids.

I was able to attend the kids' school functions that I couldn't make prior to my injury. These activities included field trips, school plays, school sporting events such as track and field day, and even the dreaded parent-teacher conferences.

When Brad was in second grade, his class went on a field trip to ride on a buckboard pulled by horses to tour a farm. The opportunity arose for me to go along with the kids and the teacher to help chaperone. The field trip was scheduled for just 2 months after my first back surgery. I thought this would be a good chance for me to get some fresh air considering I had been housebound pretty much since my surgery.

Brad and I arrived at his school the day of the field trip, and I met all the other parents going along with the kids. The problem was, all the other 6 parent chaperones were mothers, no fathers.

My first thought was, *Oh no*. Not that I have a problem with mothers, but I was thinking this might be a long day listening to them share their war stories.

I wasn't totally disappointed because Brad's second grade teacher was a man. I kind of thought he was thinking the same as I was: Oh boy, what's the gossip du jour going to be?

At the time, I must have been one of the first stay-at-home dads, and I didn't like having that thought. To me, it was kind of insulting to my pride and manhood. Nowadays, stay-at-home dads are very common, and I don't think it has the stigma that it did once.

Another brilliant idea of mine during this time was to go out and buy a new Yamaha 450cc street motorcycle.

Being in the mental and physical condition I was in at the time, taking 16 narcotic tablets a day, pretty much having a numb left leg, and not having all my faculties, what could possibly go wrong?

I would give Brad rides to and from school and rides to and from his sports practices.

On my own, I would travel down the freeway at high speeds, take long winding rides through the mountains, and even take rides at night, all under the influence of narcotics.

Once in a long while, I would make a good decision. One of those decisions was to park my motorcycle in the garage permanently.

After I parked the motorcycle and reflected a bit on what I had done on it before it was parked, I felt blessed that nothing had happened to me or anyone else. I must have had a Guardian Angel looking after me, considering the potential disasters that could have occurred while riding.

The cause of my numb/dead left leg was a signal that another spinal disc was going out. This would eventually lead to my subsequent surgery in 2007 - more on this later in the book. Hey, lucky me!

Being a stay-at-home dad allowed me a lot of free time to think about my future career.

I had always been interested in Real Estate, especially with the home prices in California, so I decided to study and apply for a California Real Estate Salesperson License.

I successfully studied and passed the California Real Estate Exam and became a licensed real estate agent in 2002.

After studying and passing the exam, I became even more interested in the real estate business and wanted to learn everything possible to be successful.

Shortly after acquiring my RE License, I had to decide if I wanted to stay with FedEx. If I chose to stay with them, it would have to be in a different capacity.

Staying with FedEx would most likely be me taking an office position, and I had never had an "office" job. FedEx offered me a position processing the paperwork for international packages at a reduced salary, and I seriously considered it but ultimately decided not to accept the position.

Chris and I made the choice to part ways with FedEx and get some additional training applicable to my real estate license.

My thinking was, "now is my chance to start a new profession," and one that I already had studied, completed, and obtained a license for.

FedEx offered me some financial assistance toward retraining which I accepted. They paid for my tuition so that I could get the certification for Mortgage Financing. Not only would this education benefit my real estate career, but it would also be another revenue stream for me.

I've always enjoyed finance, not to the point of sitting in an office and crushing numbers, but to know the financial needs of potential homebuyers and homeowners who want to refinance, so I enrolled in a mortgage and finance course. The course came naturally to me, and I loved the challenge of calculating people's qualifications when trying to purchase or refinance a home, finding their debt to income ratio (DTI), their loan to value ratio (LTV), and reducing their debt to qualify for a mortgage, etc.

One of my best traits is the ability to talk to just about anyone and feel comfortable doing so.

I had a good run in the real estate and mortgage business for almost 2 years, and then BOOM! My back required another level to be fused, and so in June of 2004, I went under the knife again and all the rehabilitation time that goes with it.

Now, going through another 18 months of rehab so close to completing my first rehab period was a major blow to my mental state.

The second surgery began a very dark period for me because I was really starting to feel sorry for myself.

I felt self-pity because of all I'd been through, taking opiates every day, not being the person I used to be physically and mentally, and having deteriorating relationships with family and friends. I was becoming an emotional wreck.

It got to the point when Chris left for work, I would walk her out, watch her drive off down the road, and then start to weep. It became so bad that Chris wouldn't know if I would be dead or alive when she got home.

During this dark period, I attempted to return to my Real Estate & Mortgage business. One of the best blessings during this time was when my friend Jeff Schmidt wanted to explore the possibility of purchasing a new home.

Jeff and his family had lived in Mira Mesa for over 30 years, and now that all the kids were grown up and had moved out, he and his wife wanted to see what options were out there.

I met Jeff when I was 18 years old and joined his recreational softball team known as the "Crabs." Jeff and I immediately became good friends and have continued that friendship for over 40 years. If I were in real trouble and only had one phone call to make, the call would be to him.

Jeff and his wife wanted to escape life in suburbia and go rural. Since their desirable properties were in the undeveloped area of San Diego County, Jeff always offered to drive his big Ford F-350, 4-wheel drive truck to view potential properties. This worked out well because most of the properties he wanted to view were generally down a washboard, bumpy road or even worse.

The most difficult chore for me was getting in and out of his big-ass truck. During nearly the next 2 years and after viewing over a hundred listings, the Schmidt's found their perfect dream home in Ramona.

Ironically, their new home is located on the same road where many of my relatives owned land in the 1960s. As a kid, my family and I would go up to their properties and ride dirt bikes, shoot guns, and I even learned how to shoot a bow and arrow there.

These trips were tremendously helpful to my mental health during the 2 years of looking, and I don't think Jeff realizes how therapeutic they were to me. At this point in time, I was at the lowest and deepest point of my addiction and under the most potent influence from opiates.

It got me outside for most of the day, which was a novelty for me at this point, and we would always stop for lunch. Most of the time, our lunch was at "The Boll Weevil" restaurant. Other times it might be at a local casino on one of the many nearby Indian reservations.

I don't think Jeff ever realized how much these days out meant to me.

Thank you so much, Jeff!

Jeff and his wife and my other 99% of clients were great, but I also dealt with the polar opposite type. I sold the home of one of my clients when they moved away from San Diego. When returning to San Diego, they asked me to assist them in finding a new house.

The wife would fly into town from New York, leaving her husband at home to continue to work. She and I would spend the next few days checking out potential homes. The problem was she didn't really know what she or her husband wanted. So, my task of finding them a new home was a difficult one.

One day, she would want to look at the biggest house possible; the next day, we would be looking at a tiny beach house. The day after that, it would have to be a newer home, and then it would be a fixer-upper. You get the picture.

When the husband was able to fly out with her, the criteria would change again. The challenge was that we could never go out to view listings until the Ohio State Football game was over. Then I would have to take them out to lunch or at least a Starbucks before heading out to view their listings of the day.

I worked with them for almost a year, trying to find them a suitable home. The husband soon joined her in the indecisiveness, and the situation became very frustrating for me. We finally came to a mutual agreement to part ways without ever finding them a new home to purchase.

This was another major mental defeat for me, and something I've never gotten over. The amount of lost time, the amount of money, and all the effort on my part that was seriously wasted.

If they read this book, they'll know who I'm talking about.

Chapter 11: My First Vacation Post Surgery

Now it's time to move on to some of my trials and tribulations while being an active drug addict.

While recovering from my first surgery, there was a lot of adjusting that occurred so that I could function somewhat normally. I had to learn how to maneuver everything all over again, getting in and out of bed, going up and downstairs, getting in and out of a car, tying my shoes, getting in and out of a chair, and all the other movements you do throughout the day. I had to retrain my brain and body to do everything a new way.

One of the most significant reality checks was realizing I would never be the same. Most of my strengths, both physical and mental, had now become weaknesses, and the sooner I accepted that, the better off I'd be. Easier said than done. This new mindset was depressing and very demoralizing for me.

In the spring of 2002, about 6 months after my first surgery, Chris, Brad, and I went on a road trip to San Francisco. Erica was planning on going with us, but she and her mother decided that she wouldn't be going the morning we were leaving. I was disappointed, to say the least, but I think Brad was more upset. Brad really loves his sister and was looking forward to the trip with her.

At that time, we had a Volkswagen Eurovan, which had a bench seat, table, TV, and rear-facing seats. The kids loved playing games at the table or watching a movie while on road trips. With the Eurovan, getting in and out was easy compared to getting in and out of a sedan, and it had much more room in it to stretch out.

This was my first getaway since the surgery and I really didn't know what to expect or how I would do.

Chris booked a brand-new hotel in San Francisco called the Argonaut for a week. It was located right on Fisherman's Wharf. The trip ended up being fantastic and tremendously helpful to my mental health, along with Chris and Brad's.

I'll never forget on our way back to San Diego, we stopped by Universal Studios in Los Angeles to catch up with some of Chris's friends from England.

We had booked a Sheraton hotel, and when we arrived, we required some assistance with our bags. That's where we met the bellman who helped us with our luggage. He was an older, very tall, and strong-looking gentleman.

While he was bending over, unloading the cases out of the back of the van, his shirt raised above his waist, and I saw a scar identical to one I now had from the surgery. I asked him about his scar, and he told me all about the surgery he had many years earlier.

Listening to the description of his surgery, it seemed very similar to the one I just had with only one exception; his surgery was only a one-level fusion compared to mine being a 2-level fusion. My take-away from our conversation was there is hope for me; look how he lifts and moves these suitcases around. That was nearly 20 years ago, and I remember it like it was yesterday. He became my inspiration.

Even at the beginning of my drug use, it didn't take long for my demeanor to change and even my whole personality. I no longer had much patience and often had unexplained outbursts. It's just the nature of the beast when you become an addict.

Chris had always insisted on taking an annual vacation to some destination. Brett and Erica were always invited to join our yearly vacations, and most of the time, they would, but sometimes, there was a conflict in schedules, and they wouldn't be able to go.

Over time, it seemed like they had more and more scheduling conflicts so that it would be just Chris, Brad, and me.

I think Brett and Erica were acutely aware that the potential existed for me to have a meltdown or confrontation at any moment about anything. They knew I didn't care, and I didn't care who witnessed it, so chose not to go. Brad's good friend Chad came along with us on a few trips when Brett and Erica didn't go. Chad was never a problem and he provided Brad with some company other than just Chris and me. Hanging with mom and dad could get boring, demanding, and overwhelming.

When I was younger, I frequently went on vacation to Lake Tahoe to go skiing, hiking, or just to play in the water, which is generally chilly because the lake water is mostly melted snow. One of the good things about Lake Tahoe is after you've enjoyed your day doing outdoor activities, you could go out and enjoy the nightlife at one of the many casinos there.

Here's a little story about one of my many trips there before my injury:

One of my trips to Lake Tahoe was with 15 family members and friends to go skiing. After spending the day on the slopes, we all enjoyed the evening gambling. I wasn't having much luck at the tables that night and decided to return to the hotel. As I was crossing the 2-lane highway that runs through South Lake Tahoe, I pulled what remaining cash I had left out of my pocket and dropped one of the paper bills onto the street.

As I immediately stopped, turned around, and bent over to pick up the bill, a car's bumper went right past my head, narrowly missing me. The driver of that car thought I had passed his path and had no idea I was going to suddenly stop, therefore barely missing me. The bill I dropped was only a dollar, and I almost lost my life over it! Another reminder of how you could lose your life in an instant.

In May of 2004, Chris, Brad, and I went to Lake Tahoe and stayed at The Ridge in South Lake Tahoe near Stateline. Lake Tahoe is beautiful every season of the year. The summers are warm and perfect for watersports, and the winters are a hotbed for snow skiing, with ski resorts dotted all around the lake.

I tried so hard to participate in some of the activities and adventures the place had to offer but was restricted by the condition of my health. I remember Chris and Brad would go play racquetball, and Brad would go shoot hoops. We would take drives around the lake, and we went for a paddle boat ride on the lake.

One day we decided to go the lake beachfront to relax and watch Brad play in the water.

The beach we went to offered parasailing, and Brad really wanted to give it a go. When we inquired about booking it, we were informed that Brad wasn't heavy enough to go solo. The only option for Brad to go was for Chris or me to go with him.

The choice of which one of us would accompany Brad wasn't a tough one because Chris was an immediate "Oh hell no!"

So, it came down to me as the only option to go with Brad. I was in no physical shape or condition to be pulled by a tow line to a high attitude with Brad attached to me, but since I felt like I had already lost the ability to be a good father, I accepted the challenge and agreed to fly with him.

After we took off and reached our altitude, the sky was absolutely clear, and the water below was so crystal blue that the thrill of the ride kicked in. During our flight, I pointed out landmarks that I had learned from my previous trip to Lake Tahoe, such as ski resorts with their still snow-capped mountain peaks and other famous points of interest on the lake, such as Emerald Bay.

After our wonderful flight, we landed back on the beach and continued to enjoy the rest of the day.

When we returned to the Lodge that evening, I decided to take a shower. While washing my hair and rinsing, I felt a sunburn on the top of my head that I had never felt before. It really hurt. After getting out of the shower, I looked in the mirror to see how bad the burn was and realized for the first time that I was losing my hair. I had always had a full head of hair and never imagined I would start to go bald, even though I did start going gray when I was about 16. The gray hair used to come in handy when I was young because I was one of the few who could go and buy beer!

Throughout the rest of our stay, my pain continued to worsen. I knew the kind of pain I was having wasn't anything good, and over the next couple of days, the pain became so bad I was in tears. At this point, we decided to head back home, which was an 11-hour road trip, and I was in no position to drive.

At that moment, I didn't realize that this trip would be one of my highlights for the next several years. The pain, mainly in my left leg, was so bad it felt like my leg was broken in two, and the two "broken" bones were rubbing against each other, causing unbearable pain.

We started the more than 500-mile drive home with Chris at the wheel of our Honda Passport SUV. As I lay down on the back row of the Passport, I couldn't for the life of me get into a position that would relieve my pain.

I would get comfortable for a moment or two, but then the sharp tearing of the muscles, bone rubbing against bone pain would rear its ugly head and bring me to tears. Even with the narcotics, I had little to no relief from the pain.

Can you imagine yourself being on a drive for over 500 miles with a young boy as your co-pilot and a whining, crying, grown man in the back seat, and there was nothing you could do to ease my pain or shorten the drive?

Chris was the real hero on this mission to get home, driving all the way, only stopping once to refuel and grab some fast food. After making the 10+ drive home, I was in so much pain that I couldn't tolerate it anymore. As soon as we got home, we dropped Brad with his grandparents and headed straight to Sharp Memorial Hospital to seek help.

Upon arriving and being admitted to the emergency room, the ER physician was at a loss of what to do, so he injected me with a large dose of Morphine. The injection gave a little relief, but not much. As the doctor continued to identify the cause of my pain and discussed my previous back surgery, he concluded that he couldn't help me any further. He felt the best plan of attack was to hit me again with another dose of Morphine, instruct me to make an appointment with my surgeon ASAP and then send me on my way. Then, right before I was discharged from the emergency room, he decided to inject me with a third dose of Morphine. That made a total of three shots of morphine within an hour and a half, and man, I felt like I was parasailing once again, having an out of body experience.

On the way back home after leaving the hospital, I became so nauseous from the Morphine to the point that Chris had to pull the car over to the side of the road so I could vomit, and boy did I vomit. I could still taste the Morphine that was oozing out of the inside of my cheeks and in my mouth. It's a taste that I'll remember for a lifetime.

After clearing my stomach of everything on the side of the road, we continued to head home. By now, it was about 3 am, and Chris had had enough drama for the day, so when passing the neighborhood elementary school on the way home and approaching the 3-way stop sign, she just blew straight through the sign without hesitation! It had to be one of the worst days for

Chris, as it consisted of making the 10+ hour drive from Tahoe, which wasn't the easiest of drives, then spending the wee hours of the morning in the emergency room waiting for me to be treated.

Chapter 12: A Letter from My Daughter Erica

My father had an addiction, and because of his addiction, it created great affliction. I grew up resenting my father not only for the pain he caused me but the empty feeling he left in my heart. I know this wasn't the person he was raised to be and especially not the person he wanted to become, but years of drug dependency created a person that no one could relate to or even wanted to be around.

Lately, he has done his best to make amends for the deep scars he has inflicted on me and our family. Sometimes I wonder if it is too little too late, but at the end of the day, all I want is to be close to my father and have a good relationship with him.

These days I feel like I'm learning who he is all over again. I love who he is now and feel like we can finally move past our differences and learn to love each other for who we actually are instead of what his addiction made of us.

Erica

Unfortunately for Erica, her memories of me being her father and living in the same house are very limited due to her young age at the time of the divorce.

After the divorce was finalized, there was animosity toward me from Brett and Erica's mother and her family. Most of the animosity came from how quickly I had met Chris and got on with my life.

Erica was 4 at the time, a very impressionable age, and it's my opinion that she was sometimes used as a pawn to get back at me. When this happened, it always caused a lot of tension, not only between Erica and me, but for many other family members on both sides. I don't want to sound like I'm berating her mother or her family, but I think kids are often used as pawns during and after a divorce, which is sad.

Fortunately, I have lots of great memories of Erica when she was young, and I've always taken care to be the best father possible.

When Chris and I bought a house in the Scripps Ranch area of San Diego, we would have Erica and Brett every Thursday night and had to get them to school early Friday morning. At the time, they went to two different schools that had two different start times. I would drop off Brett at his school and take Erica to my father's house until her school start time. One of our favorite memories was hanging out at grandpa's house, where she always had peanut butter toast and chocolate milk for breakfast.

When we took them back to their mother after a weekend stay, Erica would always have to have a bowl of mint chocolate-chip ice cream. The funny thing was, she never wanted to eat it until we were in the car and driving back to her house.

I would like to share a story about something extraordinary and scary that happened to Erica when she was a baby.

When Erica was only about 2 months old, her mother laid her down for an afternoon nap in her crib. After a short time, I went to look in on her, and her appearance didn't look normal, almost comatose. I tried to get her to react to my touches, but she was unresponsive.

I instantly decided to rush her to the hospital, which was only 5 minutes from our house. Her mother didn't react with the same urgency but agreed it was best to go and have her checked out.

Upon arrival at the emergency room, Erica was immediately taken back to a room for diagnosis by a very young doctor. This young doctor made an immediate request for a spinal tap.

Scared to death and not really knowing if this doctor knew what he was doing, we decided to proceed with the spinal tap. The minute the spinal fluid was withdrawn, he knew that the fluid didn't look right and had the sample rushed off to the lab for diagnosis. Within minutes, the sample results were back, and it was determined that Erica had spinal meningitis.

She was immediately checked into the hospital, put in a private room, and put into a medically induced coma to reduce the swelling of her brain.

For the next few days, her condition was touch and go. Erica ended up staying in the hospital for a week. For that week, I never left her side, spending the nights in the room with her. I wouldn't have had it any other way.

From that moment on, I felt we had a special bond. She has always had a special place in my heart, and I realize just how lucky we are to still have her with us.

Thank God!

Chris and I always took an annual vacation with all the kids, but as the years went by, Erica's participation became less and less frequent. On more than one occasion, she would back out of a trip at the very last moment, and I mean the very last moment. For example, we would be planning to leave at 9:00 in the morning, and we would get a call at 8:30am saying "she wasn't feeling well" or some other lame excuse. This was disappointing to Chris and me and to her brothers, especially Brad, who totally idolizes her. Brad could never understand how or why this would happen.

Now for Erica's biggest disappointment in me. First, let me explain that I love all three of my kids the same, with my whole heart, not one more than the other, but all the same. I've always tried to illustrate this to them, and hopefully, they all understand, but sometimes emotions run high and make it feel that that's not the case.

In February of 2019, there was a massive scheduling conflict. Brad, Erica's younger brother, was graduating from the United States Airforce Bootcamp in San Antonio, TX, on the very same day as her wedding rehearsal dinner in San Diego. What are the chances? I didn't want to miss either of them.

I explained my predicament to Erica, hoping she would understand my decision to attend both Brad's graduation and then her wedding the next day, which meant missing the rehearsal dinner.

Our plan was to fly to San Antonio on Thursday to share Brad's graduation with him on Friday morning and then fly out to San Diego Friday evening. With the timing of these two special events so close to each other, there was no way I would be able to attend the rehearsal dinner back in San Diego.

Once we were checked into the hotel where the wedding was taking place, I immediately reached out to Erica to let her know that we were there and that we were really looking forward to the wedding. She insisted on me going over to her room to see her, and I did. It appeared everything was good, and excitement was in the air. We chatted for a bit, and then I returned to my room.

The wedding the next day was a great success. Erica was so beautiful, and I delivered my "father of the bride" speech without a hitch.

At that point, I thought I had successfully attended both once-in-a-lifetime events, with the only exception of missing the rehearsal dinner. Apparently, I was completely wrong and would only find out a few years later.

I found out through a friend how devastated Erica was with me missing the rehearsal dinner. It turns out that Erica's aunt shared

Erica's feelings with a good friend of mine, knowing it would get back to me, with the sole purpose of making me feel worse than I already did.

At that time, I was unsure if Erica's husband Jonatan knew the whole story about my addiction. The topic hasn't ever come up in the years since. His lack of knowledge about my addiction probably falls in the category of "my dirty little secret."

Just a few months ago, out of the blue, Erica called me and was a little emotional. The reason for her call was to tell me how she feels about me now. She went on to say how much she loves me and appreciates all that I've done for her, how I never missed visitation time with her and her brother Brett.

Erica, I love you more than anything, and I feel our relationship is better now than any other point in our lives. Thank you for sticking around and not giving up on me!

Love you, Erica and Jonatan!

Chapter 13: A Few Perks of Chris's Job

In 2003, Chris started working as a Creative Director for a resort company, which gave her the benefit of booking timeshares pretty much anytime she wanted to.

We would go several times a year to a Marriott, Hilton, or other property for a week and sometimes longer. Being in the business, she was able to book these fantastic properties at a ridiculously low price. What a perk!

These little trips would be all over the country. Some of the resorts we stayed at were in Palm Springs, Lake Tahoe, Las Vegas, Virginia, North Carolina, New York, and many in Florida.

Palm Springs was always a favorite for everyone. It was only a short 2-hour drive from San Diego. Sometimes, Chris would book 2 or 3 units at the same time so family and friends could come and stay comfortably. We always had a great time.

On several occasions, Chris and the kids would come out and stay 3 or 4 days, and when they left to go home, my buddies would come and hang out for the remainder of the stay.

On one trip, Chris booked villas in Orlando for 2 weeks. Chris's good friend from England and her family met us there.

My birthday is on September 17th, and Chris would always book a timeshare stay for my birthday. Most of the time, it would be at one of the properties in Palm Desert, a town just east of Palm Springs.

Chris had another great perk with her job: getting tickets to special events. Most of these would be sporting events. Her company did a tremendous amount of advertising with all the local sports teams and even some for teams in other cities.

Whenever she requested tickets to a game, she was always provided with at least 4. The tickets would only be for the best seats, and sometimes, they would be for a suite along with all the catered food and drink you could enjoy.

Most of the time, Chris didn't care to go to the game, so that meant I could ask 3 of my buddies to the game. Since they were only the best of the best tickets and all my buddies knew this, none of them ever hesitated in accepting my offer!

Going to the games with my buddies was a real highlight for me, especially during the 10 years of surgeries, drugs, and all the setbacks, when I was at the lowest point of my life, seriously thinking that Chris and everyone would be better off without me.

Not that I would take my own life, knowing that would be the greatest sin to my faith, but maybe a natural death somehow, or even an accidental overdose, perhaps some sort of an accident, or even possibly natural causes considering my physical and mental health condition.

Thanks to the unconditional love, support, belief in me from all my loved ones, and the blessing of God, I made it through it.

Chapter 14: The Escalation of Pain Medicine and More Surgeries

Within a few months after taking Vicodin numerous times daily, it became apparent the drug was having a minimal effect on reducing my pain.

The next narcotic prescribed was Percocet. Again, after a short time, the Percocet wasn't working for the pain. The following drug to be prescribed was Hydrocodone, and the same thing happened; after a while, I felt no relief.

Then I moved on to the drug that I would take for almost 10 years, Oxycontin. I was prescribed Oxycontin and a muscle relaxant named "Soma" to go along with it. They also prescribed Xanax. I think that was to help me from going crazy

This narcotic combination would become my drug cocktail at the doctor's direction ... and the cause of my addiction that lasted nearly 10 years.

The combination of Oxycontin and Soma is often referred to on the street as "Rich Man's Heroin." When taking Oxycontin and Soma together, their effect is the same as someone injecting Heroin; it's the same euphoria and mental state of mind.

After I was clean, I had a conversation with a pharmacist and we talked about the combination of drugs I was prescribed, including quantity and dosage, all in the name of pain management. As I spoke, I noticed he was really concentrating. Once I finished, he stated that in the pharmacy world, they called this combination of Oxy, Soma, and Xanax "The Holy Trinity … be prepared to meet your maker".

It was strange that I took the exact same number of drugs every day, but the mental and physical intensity of the drug would affect me differently from day to day. Some days, I felt like I was functioning as a normal person… or that's what I thought. The people around me weren't thinking that. I've been told there were countless times when I was incoherent. Other days, I felt like a complete down-and-out drug addict.

Once again, I should be dead, period!

Let me provide some information on the drugs I was taking.

Soma: Carisoprodol also known by the name **Soma**, is a prescription skeletal muscle relaxant. It is typically prescribed to relieve some pain caused by muscle injuries like strains and sprains, stiffness, and spasms from surgeries. It blocks the pain sensations between the nerves and the brain. At higher doses, soma can lead to a euphoric high.

Soma is a schedule 4 controlled substance under the Controlled Substance Act. The drug comes in tablet form and is taken by mouth, often several times a day when treating an injury.

Combining Soma with opioids for even a minimally short time is a quick path to addiction and is life threatening.

On many occasions, when attempting to swallow my 4-tablet narcotic cocktail, one of the Soma would unexpectedly dissolve in my mouth before I swallowed it. When this happened, it would be the worst taste in my mouth possible, and it wouldn't go away for some time.

Oxycontin: Oxycontin is a strong prescription pain medicine that contains an opioid (narcotic) that's used to manage pain severe enough to require daily round-the-clock, long-term treatment.

Oxycontin is a schedule 2 controlled substance under the Controlled Substance Act. It's a narcotic analgesic that's widely used in clinical medicine (pain management).

This narcotic and all other narcotics comes an extremely high risk for addiction and dependency.

It can also cause respiratory distress and death when taken in high doses or when combined with other substances and alcohol.

My first surgery benefitted me for almost three years until another level of my spine (L4-L5) caused so much pain that it also required a spinal fusion. Just when I think I'm almost entirely recovered from one surgery, here we go again.

This time it was only a one-level fusion, and "Dr. Lance" performed the surgery at Sharp Memorial Hospital in San Diego in June of 2004. This procedure also required cutting through the muscle mass with another 8-inch incision and implanting new hardware, titanium rods, and bolts. Dr. Lance also removed the hardware from my prior surgery during this procedure. After three years, the bone cadaver that had been previously implanted at levels L2-L4 was fused entirely, and the hardware was no longer required.

A day or so after this surgery, Dr. Lance came into my hospital room to check on my condition. I was lying in bed watching the U.S. Open golf tournament, and Dr. Lance sat down on the side of my bed to watch the golf with me for an hour or so. During this time, we discussed my surgery, what to expect during recovery, and future rehabilitation plans.

From that point on, Dr. Lance and I had a special connection. I was confident I was in good hands and felt comfortable having him as my surgeon. Little did I know at the time that he would be cutting into me again three years later.

My rehabilitation period was expected to take up to 18 months. As it turned out, and with the experience of having already gone through major back surgery, I was able to get as good as I was going to get in about 8 months. I knew exactly how to push myself to the limit when it came to physical therapy. The recovery time was also shortened by going into aqua therapy straight after the surgery.

Unfortunately for me, in the Spring of 2007, my back was giving me more trouble. With my experience and knowing when something wasn't feeling right, I knew I was in trouble again.

I scheduled an appointment to go and see Dr. Lance once again to decide what type of treatment was needed to get me up and running again, so to speak.

We had a detailed Q&A during this appointment, and he conducted a few mobility tests on me. He said that the best way to tell what was going on with my back was to have an MRI performed.

I was hoping and praying that the MRI findings wouldn't require another surgery, but I knew in my heart that wouldn't be the case, and I was ultimately correct, making it my third major spinal surgery within 6 years.

After my first and second surgeries, where I was cut wide open, Chris had started researching to see if there were any new alternatives. She attended a few seminars at hospitals in the San Diego area, where she learned about new spinal surgical procedures. These were already being used in Europe and were beginning to be performed here in the U.S. These seminars were hosted by local neurosurgeons, describing the new "minimally invasive" surgery procedures and how these new techniques would significantly reduce the recovery time.

Before going to meet with Dr. Lance to discuss the findings of my recent MRI and what options were available for my treatment, Chris said, "If Dr. Lance isn't trained in this new minimally invasive surgery procedure, we'll seek another surgeon."

After the MRI was completed, we scheduled an appointment and went back to Dr. Lance to follow up on the findings. Right up until the appointment day, Chris and I agreed about our requirement for this new surgery technique.

When Dr. Lance came into the examination room and reviewed my MRI, he told us what needed to be done to correct my back. He explained that another level of my spine was damaged to the point of no return and needed to be fused—this time at the level of L5-S1.

Dr. Lance went on to explain that he had just recently returned from Europe, where he had been trained on a new surgical procedure currently being performed called "minimal invasive spinal surgery." Our prayers had been answered!

He explained that he only had to make two small incisions about three inches long each, one along each side of the spine with this type of surgery. There would be no cutting through the muscle mass, and they could still implant new and remove the old hardware, such as rods, screws, etc., required for a successful recovery. Minimally invasive surgery would also reduce my recovery period to approximately 6 months.

He felt I was a perfect candidate for this type of surgery, considering my age, my health, and the current condition at this level of my spine.

That's when Chris and I looked at each other, and we could see the pleasure and optimism in each other's eyes. Finally, a little bit of good news!

The doctor also informed us that he would be implanting flexible rods in my spine, significantly reducing the risk of other levels of my spine going out and needing medical attention.

The flexible rods allow the spine to bend at a particular level where they're implanted, reducing the amount of torque pressure on the spine while bending over. In my previous two surgeries, the rods hadn't been flexible. With the installation of flexible rods, it meant I would have a little more ability to bend over without putting extra stress and torque on my spine like the nonflexible rods did.

Dr. Lance and other neurosurgeons believed rods that don't flex contribute to the cause of different levels being damaged to the point of requiring surgery.

Here is an interesting fact describing the pressure ratio that's placed on your back when you lift items:

"It operates on a 10:1 ratio. Lifting an object weighing 10 pounds puts 100 pounds of pressure on your lower back. When you add the 105 pounds of the average human torso, you see that lifting a 10-pound object actually puts 1,150 pounds of pressure on the lower back."

So please always practice safe and proper lifting techniques. You don't want to go through what I've had to go through.

A large percentage of the residual pain that I have and will always have comes from scar tissue that has developed post-surgery due to the surgeon having cut through the main torso muscles and nerves. The build-up of scar tissue is significantly reduced with minimally invasive surgery.

Dr. Lance performed my third surgery in August of 2007. He removed the hardware from my previous surgery since that level was also completely fused, cleaned up what scar tissue he could, and installed the new flexible rods and the screws.

By this time, my physician at the pain management facility was prescribing me 240 Oxycontin, 240 Somas, and 90 Xanax a month. I guess the Xanax was just for shits and giggles!

One time, we were going to travel to England. Before leaving, I was at the pain management facility for my regular visit along with my wife to discuss my meds when the physician's assistant suggested prescribing a three-month supply of each medication, Oxycontin, Soma, and Xanax. That amounted to a prescription of 720 Oxycontin, 720 Soma, and 270 Xanax!

My wife blew a gasket and said, "Hell no, are you mad? He won't be needing that amount. Just keep Greg on his regular one-month prescription."

In today's world, the opiate crisis has been finally recognized, and physicians now would never be allowed to prescribe the quantity of narcotics that were being prescribed to me.

One of the things that became apparent to me was once acquaintances or friends found out I had access to prescribed narcotics, some of them would want to become a bit closer and much friendlier. They would approach me and ask if they could have a tablet or two or buy a tablet or two.

Their excuses or reasons for wanting tablets ran the whole spectrum, and I think I heard them all …

"This or that is hurting."

"I have a migraine and a tablet or two would really help."

"I just want to catch a buzz and have a nice relaxing day."

The excuses and reasons were endless and on and on and on they went. You would sure see their other side when you told them "NO." Some of the excuses I gave for not giving them any of my drugs were "I'm almost out," "The Doc hasn't refilled my script yet," or just "Sorry, no can do."

In the beginning of my pain management (drug use), my cocktail of Oxycontin and Soma did somewhat numb and mask the pain, but the pain never ever went completely away.

Here's a quote from a hematologist describing and understanding "chronic pain" better than most doctors and specialists.

"Chronic pain patients hide their pain so well. You can't go by how they look on the outside. They must learn how to function with pain; you can't just roll around on the floor all day screaming in agony. Medical personnel in hospitals don't even realize this. A chronic pain patient can function with a pain level that would incapacitate any other person."

For the next several years, I took 16 tablets a day. My schedule was 2 Oxycontin and 2 Soma at 8:00 am, again at noon, another dose at 4:00 pm, and then I would wait as long as I could before taking the last 2 Oxycontin and 2 Soma for the day, generally around 10:00 pm.

When I went out for long periods of the day, I would prepare my narcotic cocktails by placing 2 Oxycontin and 2 Soma into a small piece of aluminum foil and folding it up, placing it into my shorts or trouser coin pocket. I could have 2 or 3 of these little goodie bags with me on some days. I became very good at taking my tablets without anyone noticing and being under the radar, I thought. Sometimes, I would even have to swallow them without any water or other liquid.

Here's one example:

Our family trip to England consisted of my sister, Vicki, my brother-in-law, David, Brad, Chris, and myself. During the vacation, we also planned on taking the train from Kent, England, through the Channel Tunnel, also known as the "Chunnel", that goes underneath the English Channel to Paris, France.

When the train arrived in Paris, we had to go through the French Customs checkpoint. It was only then that I realized I had in my possession the narcotics that I always carried with me wrapped in silver foil, not in prescription bottles, so I could take my 4 daily doses. Luckily, I was allowed entry without any problem, but if the Customs had searched me and found the narcotics, I would probably still be imprisoned in France! Somebody was definitely looking out for me.

Chapter 15: My Dirty Little Secret

The ability to hide my addiction is something I learned very quickly. Unfortunately, the people around me also had to learn how to deal with it and hide it.

I think the reason we hid it was because of the shame, the embarrassment, and the consequences if this secret came out.

The stigma that goes along with being associated with a person who has an addiction has far-reaching consequences. For me, it didn't matter that the addiction was from a prescribed regimen rather than street drugs; the stigma was still there.

As a recovering opioid addict, I can often recognize people who have an alcohol or drug addiction, even people who have recovered.

Although this hasn't always been the case, as I'll explain, here's a perfect example of a "dirty little secret":

When I was a teenager, I had a girlfriend, and I became close to her family, especially her father. My girlfriend and I dated for many years, so I spent a lot of time around him. I thought I knew him really well, but little did I know, her father was an alcoholic.

His drinking addiction wasn't one where he had to drink every day. But once he started drinking, he couldn't stop; he would go on a bender.

**A drinking bender is an extended period of continued excessive drinking with little food and little sleep.*

For the years leading up to me finding out about her father's dirty little secret, I worked at the neighborhood grocery store. Most Saturdays I would have to work at the grocery store, which was only about a half mile away from their house. The family had a tradition of making homemade tacos every Saturday, so they would invite me to have some of their tacos for my lunch.

When I arrived at their house, her dad was doing the cooking most of the time. On occasions, though, I would arrive as usual, but her dad was nowhere around. I would ask where he was, and the answer might be, "He's taking a nap" or "He's out running an errand." I never thought twice about their response.

I would eventually learn that her dad would be sleeping off his bender or be in the middle of his binge drinking that could last 2 or 3 days.

Her dad was born and grew up in San Diego when it was more of a town rather than a big city. He had a lot of friends and knew everybody!

Back then, there were times when he would go out drinking and not be in any condition to drive his car and make it all the way back home. He would just pull his car over to the side of the road and try to sleep it off.

On more than one occasion, a police officer would arrive to investigate the parked car and realize he knew the person asleep in the car, and it would be him.

Instead of issuing him a ticket or arresting him for intoxication, the officer would give him a ride home. He would have to retrieve his car from where he left it the following day. This kind of special treatment wouldn't happen in today's world.

Other times, when he couldn't drive and didn't go home, my girlfriend, her two sisters, along with their mother, would have to go out late at night or in the wee hours of the morning to look for him.

My girlfriend and her family were able to keep the "dirty little secret" of his addiction from me for years. It really wasn't until he made the decision to seek help that I was brought into the loop about his drinking addiction.

I believe they probably would have tried to continue hiding it from me as long as possible if it hadn't been for him having to check into the Veteran's Affairs (VA) hospital for help with his alcohol addiction. He remained in the VA for several weeks, seeking sobriety and continuing with AA meetings. After he completed his journey to sobriety, he never had another drink for the remainder of his life, and he also sponsored other alcoholics. Congratulations!

I've thought a lot about how it must have been for my girlfriend and her sisters growing up with an alcoholic, always having to hide it, going out to look for their father in the middle of the night in their pajamas, covering up for his mistakes when he was drunk. These are mental scars that they'll have for the rest of their lives.

I never, ever thought that one day I would be putting my own family through the same mental anguish that they had to endure growing up.

Unfortunately for my family, that's precisely the position I put them in. From my standpoint, I was able to see firsthand the pain, agony, embarrassment, and shame that they endured, all because of me and my drug addiction.

My family members went to great lengths to keep the "dirty little secret" about their husband, dad, brother, and uncle.

There's definitely a stigma that goes along with being an addict. People have their own impressions of addicts, and their thoughts are many.

A few of their concerns might be:

"I can't trust him."

"He's not in his right mind."

"I'm not having him drive my kids anywhere."

"I can't let my kids go over there to play with drugs in the house."

"It's too bad, but I really don't want him in my house."

The excuses people make so they don't have to socialize with me would be endless if they became aware of my addiction. I think that's why family members of addicts do what they do to keep the "dirty little secret." I know it would have been a game-changer for my family and the relationships with their friends.

People will say that it wouldn't have, but they would be lying to you. They can't help but only want to protect their loved ones whenever possible, and I totally understand that. That's why my family circled the wagons to protect my image as well as theirs.

With my addiction, there were a lot of people who knew the history of my back surgeries and understood the pain that was associated with it. What they didn't realize was the fact that I was consuming 16 narcotic tablets a day. I'm sure if they had known, it would have played a significant role in how my relationships would have carried on.

The following is an example of how easily it was to keep my "dirty little secret" from Chris's parents.

After Chris became a U.S. citizen, she was able to sponsor her parents' immigration to the United States. Another drawn-out process the INS puts you through. In order to be a sponsor, that person must be a blood relative.

Her sister was also living in San Diego at the time but wasn't a U.S. citizen and had no intention of becoming one at that time, so it was up to Chris to be her parents' sponsor.

After much time and expense, her parents finally moved to America and were awarded their "permanent legal resident" status.

Once they moved to the U.S., they purchased a home 4 houses up the street from us in San Diego.

For the next 7 years, they lived right up the street and didn't have a clue about my addiction. Since they were unaware of my drug addiction, they had no idea how it was affecting my marriage to their daughter and how it was affecting all the kids' childhood.

They knew of my need to take pain medicine, but they had no idea what and how much I was taking. They didn't learn all the facts until I started to kick the habit and recover from the drugs. My addiction secret was kept hidden from them for 7 years.

I'm sure a lot of people reading this book currently know or have known a person, even a family member, whom they've had to cover up for. Someone who has an addiction and hides their own "dirty little secret."

Chapter 16: Mind Reading in the Waiting Room

As I wrote this book, my goal was to have it published and ready for distribution on the monumental day of January 1st, 2022, which marks my 10th year of being narcotic-free.

It has been very tough to write and reflect on the last 20 years of my life. Reliving all the pain and suffering I have inflicted on everyone around me. Not to mention the pain and suffering I was put through.

At times, I had to just stop and walk away from the writing. At other times I would find myself weeping uncontrollably. There were even occasions when I could laugh at some of my experiences during the 20 years of addiction and sobriety.

I can say firsthand, having been through the whole gamut of so-called "treatment" for pain management, that most of the blame lies with the medical profession. The choices of care and treatment that are professionally suggested and prescribed are not always in the patient's best interest.

When I had my injury, I wanted to have faith that the medical professionals had my best interest at heart. Unfortunately, I had to learn the hard way; that's not always the case.

I had no idea about the path I would eventually be on for the next 10 years. First of all, I never dreamt I would become a drug addict. Again, it really wasn't a choice I had at the time, but it was basically my only choice to try to survive.

I remember when I went for my pain management appointments, the waiting room at these facilities would be completely full most times. When called to make an appointment, it was sometimes challenging to get booked in because of the volume of patients these physicians would see daily.

When I was waiting in the lobby for my appointment, I would look around at all the other patients and try to sum them up. I would think about what their injury might be or what was the cause for them to be at the pain management facility. I would think about how their home life was going.

These were some of the other thoughts I had while observing my fellow patients:

I wonder how long they've been taking pain drugs

Have they lost everything already due to the drug use?

How could that person still have a job?

Does that person still have a roof over their head or are they just renting a room from someone?

I wonder who that person is with the patient?

What drugs are they on and how much are they taking compared to me?

It was apparent that some of them had already gotten to the point of losing their marriage, their relationship with their kids, their home, anything and everything that was important. I think their only goal now was to get a new prescription so they could replenish their inventory.

"A drug addict always knows exactly how many pills they have at all times."

I really took this opportunity to evaluate my current situation because I knew for sure that I didn't want to become one of them and another casualty of the drugs. I knew in my heart just how blessed I was at that moment and that my future was entirely up to me.

The more significant percentage of people who were in my same situation weren't as blessed as I was and didn't have the choices I had.

Not all of my observations would be the same for all the patients waiting to be seen by the doctor. Some of the patients might have suffered a recent injury and have no idea what their road was going to look like for them in the future. I'm sure most of the recently injured people had a lot of optimism for a complete recovery.

That was my state of mind when I first got injured. Even though my back injury was a major injury, I had optimism for a complete recovery and a return to normalcy. As I continued through my years of setbacks, other surgeries, and more and more pain medications in the form of opioids, I lost my optimism.

I knew just by looking at them who was a newbie and who was a hardcore patient who had been on pain management treatment for years, just as I had been.

Just looking at the others, you could see the hope and optimism in the faces of the newbies, and you could see the faces of the veterans of treatment who had lost any hope and optimism of never getting better. You could see in their faces the depression, loss of hope, and the lack of interest in life.

It was a look I became way too familiar with. Over time, it was the same look that I wore, and would have to see every time I looked in the mirror. Quite often, I would think, this can't possibly be me I'm looking at.

I felt like I had so much love and support from my family and friends. If given a chance to get off the meds, the love and support would be there for me.

I also realized there would soon come a point in time if I didn't try to help myself sooner than later, that the love and support would go away. I would end up being just like one of those other patients I would see in the waiting room who had already lost everything.

The fear of this happening to me ended up being the deciding factor for me to initiate the end of my pain management, or drug use. Thank God I had the love, support, and prayers to make the decision to quit when I did.

This might seem strange to hear, but now that I'm approaching the 10-year milestone and thinking about all the other injuries I could have suffered or the diseases that could have affected my life, I consider myself lucky to be alive.

Chapter 17: Going Off the Deep End

It wasn't long after I started my pain management regimen that I began to notice a change in my attitude. I became easily upset, wouldn't have any patience, and lost my temper a lot quicker than I ever did before.

I realized the people around me were quickly becoming aware of my new persona. When Chris and I would try to "discuss" my new attitude, the conversation would always end up going south very quickly. I would outright completely deny it, knowing all the time that it was true.

It's tough for me to admit to being an asshole who had frequent outbursts. The thing about it is, 99% of the time, my outbursts were over something so minor and stupid. Sometimes they were about nothing at all.

Ultimately, I learned that narcotics were a big reason I experienced so many changes in my personality. Besides my behavior, these changes included my appearance with the loss of some of my hair and the breakdown and decay of some of my teeth.

When I was at the dentist one day, we started talking about the sudden deterioration of my teeth. Dr. Charles explained to me that when people are on narcotics, many of them suffer tooth decay. The decay and destruction are similar to that of a meth addict.

Narcotics destroyed some of my teeth the same way as methamphetamine because it caused me to have cottonmouth. The cottonmouth got to the point where I could not get enough saliva together to spit, making my mouth very dry. Because my mouth couldn't produce enough saliva, it couldn't keep the bacteria away, hence the dental problems.

It's not a very good trade-off to have to choose between some pain relief or jeopardizing the health of your hair and teeth.

Both my mental and physical state started to spiral out of control. My meltdowns became more frequent and intense.

It soon became apparent to my family and friends that I was becoming very erratic and could go off anytime for no apparent reason.

My behavior was so unstable that my family and loved ones now say that they had to tip-toe around me for fear of me going off.

WOW! That's depressing! Not what you want the people you love to worry about.

When my personality and demeanor got to this point, I was constantly reminded of how I acted. That's when I started hating myself for becoming that person. I hated myself and didn't really understand how this had happened, but to me, there was no hope of changing. I was in a complete free fall and taking my loved ones with me.

I'm going to share a few stories about some of my actions that brought me the greatest shame. Unfortunately, there are too many to tell them all, so I'm going to talk about a few that caused me and others the most embarrassment and left the biggest mental scars.

1.

Some of my earliest outlandish behavior was at my youngest son, Brad's, sporting events. There were many times that I would say something that started a ruckus at one of his games.

I could go off at the umpire at a Little League game for making a judgment call I disagreed with.

I could go off on the referee at a youth basketball game.

I could go off on a parent who might make a comment about a play, player, team, or coach.

My behavior caused Brad, Chris, my family, and my friends irreparable shame and embarrassment through absolutely no fault of their own.

If there was an award for being the worst acting parent, I could have that trophy, at least for a few years in a row. I didn't act like this at every game, but I knew once was too much, but that didn't stop me. I'm going to go ahead and say that I'm so lucky to have gotten off the drugs when I did.

2.

On a trip to Florida with all three of the kids and Chris, we stayed at the Hilton Vacation Club in Orlando for a week. The unit we had was a large three bedroom and very spacious.

In hindsight, I probably shouldn't have agreed to go on this trip because of the pain I was in, along with my unstable mental state at the time. I wasn't in the best of health. For some reason, my left arm would just shake and shake nonstop to the point where I couldn't even hold a drink, or it would spill.

The week started out great but quickly deteriorated after a few days of heat, crowds, and all 5 of us never being separated. Tensions escalated one evening, and an argument got heated with things said that couldn't be taken back. In fact, it got so bad that my daughter, Erica, was trying to cut the trip short and fly back to San Diego.

I think I know now how tough it was for everyone to have me, the loser who demanded a lot of care and attention, tagging along to the amusement parks. Everyone had to tip-toe around me so I didn't blow a gasket.

This is a perfect example of my explosive behavior. I'm not sure how it got to this point, but it did.

I still can't help thinking that all the bullshit was my fault, and truthfully it was always my fault. In the end, we sorted it, stuck it out, and enjoyed the rest of the trip.

3.

Chris and I were at my sister Vicki's house for dinner one evening with friends Drew and Vikki. We were all sitting around having an enjoyable evening with dinner, drinks, and good conversation. I'm not sure what transpired, but for some reason, I felt like the topic of discussion was all about me. At some point, I had had enough and voiced my displeasure, and I'm sure it was in a very demanding voice.

After debating who was at fault for several heated minutes, I took it upon myself to start walking home. It would be about a 17-mile walk to get home, mostly along freeways.

It was late and dark when I started my walking adventure. As I continued my walk for nearly 2 hours and only walked approximately 6 miles, I stopped.

While I sat and rested, I rethought my decision to take this walk. I also tried to figure out what had just happened. With some remorse for leaving, I made the decision to start walking back to my sister's house.

Within a mile of my return, I notice a car's headlights approaching me, driving very slowly along the side of the freeway. Not knowing if it was the police, I hid in some bushes until the car got nearer. That's when I realized it was Chris trying to find me so she could give me a ride home.

Wow! By then, I was so happy to see her, even though I had made a real ass out of myself AGAIN, only 2 hours before!

I'll never understand what I was thinking, taking on a 17-mile walking challenge considering the bad physical shape I was in.

"Stupid is as stupid does."

4.

One year, we went to Las Vegas for my cousin's daughter's wedding. This included my sister, Vicki, her husband, David, their daughters, Amber and Ashley, along with Chris, Brad, and me. Family friends Drew and Vikki also happened to be in Vegas the same weekend just by coincidence but were not going to the wedding.

On the Friday evening before the wedding, we all decided to go to a favorite local Italian restaurant named Battista's. Since I had the VW Eurovan, we loaded into the van and headed off to dinner.

After a few hours of dining and having a lovely time, as usual, we decided to hit the Strip and have some fun. We all got back into the van and got on the freeway toward the Strip with me driving.

Not knowing exactly where we were going to go on the Strip, I repeatedly asked where we should head to. Not once did anyone ever respond to my request, as nobody could agree on a place.

I continued down the freeway and repeatedly asked again where to go, and, again, no one could agree on a spot. There was just continuing chatter and laughter coming from the back of the van. At a point of total frustration from not getting any agreement, I just pulled over to the shoulder of Interstate 15 and parked the van.

Now suddenly, I had everyone's attention, and everyone had an opinion. What I got most out of their opinions was, "What the fuck are you doing."

I tried to explain to all of them that I had asked them repeatedly, but nobody had any suggestions for where to go, and I couldn't continue to just drive down the freeway. At least that's what I thought I had done. In reality, I had exploded in a fit of uncontrollable rage. At that point, I left the van on the shoulder with everyone still in it and walked down to the next offramp.

As I walked, my head felt like a popcorn machine, just popping away, not making any sense of what just happened. When I got down to the bottom of the ramp, there was an AM/PM gas station. I walked behind the station so I could try to clear my head.

Not long after I stopped behind the station, my brother-in-law, David, came walking back toward me. I was in no mood to get lectured or have a discussion on how I behaved. I knew no one else wanted to take any responsibility for the situation or the outcome.

The discussion only lasted a few minutes until we were right in each other's faces, shouting at the top of our lungs. This was the closest I had ever come to punching David. Thank God I didn't let it go there. I somehow calmed down after a few minutes, and we had a little talk to smooth things out as good as we could, considering what had just happened.

I returned to the van and sat in the front passenger seat. By then, Chris had driven the van down to the front of the gas station. She then went on to drive everyone back to the hotel in silence; not one word was said by anyone.

The plans for going to the Strip had evaporated, and it appeared to be all my fault. Maybe I just didn't see things clearly the way I should have, and perhaps I shouldn't have become so upset so quickly. This incident really put a damper on the whole weekend, and I carried the guilt. Bummer, not again!

These are just a few examples of my bad behavior and the bad judgment, bad choices, and bad decisions I made. There are plenty more and too many to share, but some of them might come up when my loved ones provide their input. Let me describe my relationship with my brother-in-law, David.

I've known David my entire life, literally. I grew up with my cousin Randy living directly across the street from me. David was and still is my cousin's best friend. David has been on family vacations with us when we went away with my aunt, uncle, and cousin. He has always been around for as long as I can remember.

I'm not sure of the exact details, but I think he started dating my sister when he was around 21, and my sister was 17. The age difference would have never been acceptable to my family except for the fact that David was so well known and had been around the family so long. Their dating was permitted, and, sure as heck, they got married.

My sister was only 19, and David was 23 years old when they were married, and they're still married today, over 45 years later. I can truly say that David is more like a brother than a brother-in-law. Even my father considers David to be his second son. He has always supported me when needed.

Thank you, David!

Chapter 18: My Mom and Dad

My dad, Keith, will be 89 years old when this book is published. I have asked him to put into words his thoughts about me during this dire time of my life, and he opted to convey them to me verbally.

His biggest regret was his inability to help me. I could constantly see the sadness in his eyes for the pain I was going through. It wasn't only the pain, it was all the testing, the surgical procedures, the constant doctor appointments, and the effects the drugs were having on me.

He would quite often be my driver, taking me to one of my many appointments. Sometimes, it would be for an MRI, CT myelogram, epidural injection, or an EMG (electromyography). He witnessed the beating I would take from these procedures firsthand, seeing how I was before I went in for the procedure and my demeanor after the procedure. Again, I would see the sadness and frustration in his eyes and the hopelessness of his inability to help me.

My dad has always been there for me and has helped me with so many things throughout my life. He was always involved in my Little League baseball, either coaching or being on the board of directors for the league.

He brought me up, teaching me how to use my hands to repair and build things. He taught me how to repair cars and keep them maintained. He taught me how to use hand tools and power tools. His most significant influence was how to be a good man, a good father, a good husband, respect women, and generally be a good human being.

He has also saved my ass more than a few times because of certain situations I put myself in.

The following is a story my friends and I will never forget:

When I was around 12 years old, my friends and I thought throwing water balloons at cars as they drove down Navajo Road would be fun. On this one night, my friends and I filled up a bunch of water balloons and went over to the junior high school's playground.

The school's playground was just one street over from my house and on the other side of Navajo Road. The playground was situated about 20 feet above the level of the road, giving us an advantage when we threw the balloons.

After throwing several water balloons at passing cars, suddenly, we heard someone yell, "You fuckers better haul ass." When we looked to see where this shout came from, we saw 5 guys starting to run toward us.

Fortunately for us, there was an unlocked gate that we were able to go through and start running. Unfortunately for the guys running after us, they had no choice but to retreat and go back the way they came or try and catch us by going through the gate we escaped through. The guys decided to go back the way they came and tried to catch us as we ran toward my house for safety.

As my friends and I ran, some of us went in different directions. The 5 guys chasing us chose to chase down my friend Jeff and me, allowing our other friends to escape.

As they were gaining on us, we didn't have time to safely get back to my house. I was in front of Jeff by only a few seconds, and when I ran around the corner, I decided to roll underneath a car that was parked in the driveway of the corner house. With Jeff running only a few steps behind me, he saw where I went to hide and followed me under the parked car.

At this point, I thought for sure the guys chasing us saw Jeff dive underneath the car, but obviously, they didn't. When they rounded the corner, they only spotted another neighborhood kid roaming around who wasn't with us. This other kid had seen us earlier in the night and informed one of the guys where I lived.

As Jeff and I lay hiding under the car directly across the street from my house, we watched as two of the guys went to the front door of my house and rang the doorbell.

When my dad answered the door and was asked if he knew where they could find me, he immediately knew something wasn't right. Luckily for us, my dad had the foresight to send them on a wild goose chase to the San Carlos Club, where my friends and I would frequently hang out.

He thought my friends and I were in some sort of trouble because he didn't recognize either of the guys at his door, and that could only spell trouble for us if they found us. That was over 50 years ago, and my friends still talk about it and how my dad got us out of this pinch.

My relationship with both of my parents was special growing up. They would let me go and do pretty much anything I wanted to do, with a few exceptions. I never got into any serious trouble, unlike a few of my childhood friends.

When I did get into trouble, it would be for something like riding my motorcycle on the street when I was young and didn't have a license, getting busted by the police, and receiving a ticket.

Whenever I got issued a ticket, since I was a minor, I would have to go to Juvenile Court for an appearance. This would mean my dad would have to take a day off work so he could go with me. This never made him happy, which was a big disappointment to me, and the shame was punishment enough.

As I grew up, some of my friends' "great ideas" would only lead to serious trouble for them. When I'd be with them, and one of them would come up with one of these genius ideas, many times,

I'd make an excuse saying I had to be somewhere and couldn't go with them.

Many times, their idea would go south and lead them to serious consequences. I was smart enough to realize where to draw the line.

I've always had and still have so much respect for both of my parents. The last thing in the world I would want to do is cause them shame or embarrassment.

I still have my dad in my life. He's not only my father but also a great and respected friend. **Love you, Dad!**

Unfortunately, my mom, JoAnn, has been gone for over 35 years, but I respect her for all that she did in her short life and the life lessons she taught me.

My mom was diagnosed with breast cancer when she was 41 years old. Over the next 10 years of her life, she had to endure numerous surgeries, numerous rounds of chemotherapy, and other forms of therapy. Still, the cancer kept returning and moving to other parts of her body. I don't know if the treatment was worse than the disease as far as the damage that the chemo caused to her body.

She suffered through all these forms of treatment and never once complained. Her bravery over those 10 years never wavered. She never gave up hope or displayed self-pity or any signs of being scared for her future, which demonstrated how strong her faith in the Lord was right up until the day of her passing.

She was a true Braveheart. Whenever I start to think about my physical condition and want to feel sorry for myself, I remind myself of her courage, strength, and faith.

God Bless you, Mom, I miss you every day. I love you!

Chapter 19: My Journey Begins

At the beginning of October 2009, I made the decision to start the journey of kicking my drug habit. The last day for me to take my usual daily dosage of the 16-tablet cocktail was December 31st, 2009.

This gave me about 3 months to get mentally prepared between making the decision and actually starting my journey. It also gave me another 3 months to change my mind! I knew the decision that I had to make, and I wasn't going to let anything get in my way.

I felt a lot of anxiety over the next 3 months. As December 31st, 2009 approached, my anxiety only intensified. I was beginning to understand just how powerful your mind can be. I had to have the strength, motivation, support, and determination to embark on this journey for me to have a clean, drug-free life.

The 2 weeks prior to December 31st, my self-imposed deadline, was hectic. Chris and I had our secret wedding anniversary of our Las Vegas wedding, all the Christmas activities, and the family get-togethers. We also had 2 birthday celebrations for Erica on December 29th and one for Brad on December 30th.

Dr. Douglas, my pain management doctor, suggested reducing my daily consumption by 1 tablet. This reduction of just 1 tablet a month happened each month for the duration of my withdrawal.

At the time, my current daily intake was 16 tablets, 8 tablets each of Oxycontin and Soma. Theoretically, kicking 1 tablet a month, I should be completely sober in 16 months. Sounds reasonable and manageable but as I would find out, it took 2 years of living hell.

My Withdrawal

I paid the price, as well as everyone near me when each new month came around, and I had to cut another tablet out.

During my withdrawals, one moment, I would be freezing and shivering with countless blankets on me, and the next moment, I'd be burning up.

When I say, "burning up," I mean feeling like the fluids in my body were so hot they were boiling, and I felt like I was going to burn up internally.

My body ached in every nook and cranny like I had the worst flu there ever was. Every joint in my body would just ache nonstop. Quite often, I would be rolled up in the fetal position, basically just wanting to die.

Sometimes, I would become a bit delusional and confused. I thought I knew what was going on but actually had no idea what I was doing or saying. When this happened, I would become frustrated, irritable, and confrontational, taking it out on whoever was around me at that moment. I became just a mean miserable person. I was a real piece
of shit during these dire times!

The decision to get off the drugs couldn't have come at a better time for me for several reasons.

As I mentioned before, the risk of wrecking my marriage and losing my family was the most important reason.

Another significant factor probably saved my life; let me explain:

While I was on my pain management treatment, I was being prescribed 240 Oxycontin (40 mg each) and 240 Soma (350 mg each) every month. Taking 8 Oxycontin and 8 Soma a day equated to taking a total of 320 mg of Oxycontin and 2,800 mg of Soma a day. This is utterly insane by today's standard.

My high when I took the drugs was very short-lived. The exhilaration and euphoria when the drugs first kicked in only seemed to last for a few minutes, and then I would just feel dopey. You would think after the second or third dose for the day, the euphoria of the cocktail would be longer-lasting, but it wasn't. After the initial rush, I would start to come down quickly. When I felt myself coming back to earth, it wasn't a very good feeling. Once this happened, I began to watch the clock in anticipation of the next time I could take my dose of opiates.

The feeling I experienced most of the time after the initial rush was a feeling almost like my heart was barely beating, and my breaths became very shallow.

For an average person to experience these abnormal heartbeats and shallow breaths would send them into a panic and immediately want to seek medical assistance. Not for me; I never thought twice about it. If I ever mentioned the way I was feeling to anyone, they were always more concerned about it than I was. Maybe it was because, at the time, I didn't give a shit about what might happen to me, perhaps even hoping something might end this torture for me.

Unfortunately, I was one of the millions of people in the United States caught in the opiate epidemic that was ravaging America at that time. It seemed like no effort was being given at the national, state, or local level to get a grip on this epidemic. As it continued to rage out of control, it took hundreds of thousands of lives annually due to overdose.

This epidemic not only destroyed individuals' lives with addiction but also the lives of their families. It completely devastated many rural towns and big city communities until an effort began to address the opiate crisis around 2011.

When I started getting my opiate prescriptions, the doctor could prescribe what seemed like a massive quantity. They would also give the patient medication on a regular prescription pad with a few refills. This all eventually changed for the better, but the way they did it had severe and life-threatening consequences.

One of the first of many changes in the prescription process was that every licensed physician who could prescribe narcotics or any other controlled substance was required to have a DEA (Drug Enforcement Administration) number assigned to their medical license. When filling the prescription, the pharmacy must enter the DEA National Database and enter the quantity of the controlled substance being prescribed and the doctor's DEA number. This protocol allows the DEA to monitor the amount of controlled substances being prescribed by each doctor and monitors the quantity that the patient is being prescribed in the event they are attempting to manipulate the system by shopping several doctors at one time. When picking up a narcotic prescription, the pharmacy is required to scan the patient's driver's license, allowing the DEA to monitor a patient's consumption.

Another change in the policy was redesigning the prescription pads doctors would now have to use. The new design, which must have the doctor's DEA number, is printed on tamper-proof paper with an embedded hologram so that it can't be compromised or copied in any way. Also, a physician can no longer call into the pharmacy for a refill of narcotics.

Unfortunately, the decision-makers in charge of the task of addressing the epidemic started the completely wrong way. Their initial decision, and the most damning blow, was to severely reduce the quantity and frequency of narcotics that could be prescribed.

After I kicked my habit, I realized how blessed I was in the timing of my commitment to becoming drug-free. With much afterthought and reflection, I realized one thing; there would have been no way for me to have taken this challenging endeavor and survived with all the new restrictions that were put into place. The one good thing is my situation would never happen today due to the new federal quantity restrictions.

For instance, in my case, I was being prescribed 240 Oxycontin and 240 Soma per month, but now, a narcotic prescription is limited to a maximum of 7 days and, in some cases, just 3 days.

This put a patient with chronic pain in a dreadful position, as now, they're required to go to the doctor and the pharmacy more frequently. Generally speaking, the patient is in no condition to drive, either physically or mentally, because of the effects the drugs.

The problem with reducing the quantity being prescribed to an addict is that their body and their brain know precisely the amount and the strength it has been receiving each day. You wouldn't think this is a big deal, but it is. Just reducing the quantity by any amount of the previously prescribed dose comes with significant risk to the patient and possibly even death.

I know for a fact that if I was forced to make a significant reduction in the opiates I was taking every month, my body, brain, and soul would have never survived, especially after 10 years of addiction.

Addicts receiving reduced prescriptions for narcotics after the new policies were put in place had no other option than to seek other alternatives to pick up for the loss.

I repeat: Your body cannot take that amount of reduction all at one time without severe risk to your life.

Of the hundreds of thousands of people who were in this position, the large majority of them turned to street drugs. The cheapest and most available option for them at that time was heroin, and that was the path many of them chose. There are also other street drugs that people turn to, such as crack and meth. All three of these street drugs are at the top of the list for immediate addiction, and today, there's also Fentanyl.

Most insurance companies covered most of the cost for the doctor-prescribed drugs but obviously didn't cover the cost of the street drugs. This left addicts having to find other ways to fund their newfound street drug habit through illicit activities such as robbing a bank, retail store, or gas station. At this point, I guarantee you the addict isn't in their right frame of mind and isn't making their decisions clearly or wisely.

Other illicit money-grabbing activities may be stealing from a family member or a friend, running a scam of some sort, or even prostitution. Unfortunately, addicts will do anything to feed their habit. They don't care at all about the collateral damage their actions have on anyone.

Another policy change after the opiate epidemic finally gained national attention was that the DEA started monitoring and eliminating the so-called "pill mills."

A pill mill is an illegal or even sometimes legal facility that resembles a regular pain clinic or doctor's office. These facilities regularly prescribed outrageous amounts of opiates. They issued prescriptions to patients without a good medical history review, physical examination, diagnosis, medical monitoring, or any documentation for the need of such drugs.

Clients of these facilities usually receive their prescriptions by paying for them in cash. Some of these pill mills are distributing counterfeit drugs.

Some addicts would visit several pill mills, which allowed the addict to stay ahead of their needed inventory. The pill mills are a major contributor to the past and present state of the opioid epidemic.

I'm sure we have all come across someone who has been prescribed a narcotic for pain. It may have been for dental work or even a minor surgical procedure. Often, the drug that's prescribed is Vicodin.

Vicodin is a pain-reducing medicine that contains Hydrocodone. It's the next pain drug prescribed after Tylenol 3 or 4, which contains Codeine.

These lower-tier types of pain-reducing drugs are sometimes the gateway to drug experimentation. Even with these lower-tier drugs, a person can become addicted almost immediately after only a couple of days of consumption.

Before all the changes in the protocol were made to the prescribing of controlled substances, the addict would go "doctor shopping" when their addiction required more drugs than they were legally being prescribed.

The term "doctor shopping" is described as "obtaining controlled substances from multiple healthcare practitioners without the prescriber's knowledge of other prescriptions." In other words, it's when a patient manipulates the system to get extra drugs.

As you see in the next chapter, my own journey to sobriety exhausted every bit of my determination, willpower, guts, strength, support, and faith, not only for me but for all my loved ones. This is a challenge they all accepted and never wavered from, and because of that, I'm here today writing my story.

My thoughts were, I've been given an opportunity to rid myself of this addiction (thanks be to God); don't blow it because I may never get another opportunity. Basically, you have one bite at the apple, one chance to grab the brass ring, don't fuck it up.

Chapter 20: My Withdrawal

It's time for me to step up and take on the challenge of my lifetime.

This chapter will give you an idea of the process I took to become drug-free. In the back of my book, I will share my journal documenting the exact path I took to sobriety. The journal might be challenging to follow along, boring to read, and somewhat repetitive, but it illustrates how a slight reduction of these drugs took a toll on me as an addict.

My road to recovery took 2 years to complete but seemed like a lifetime.

I always made my narcotic adjustment on the first day of the month, so it was easy to forecast and keep on track. At the time, my daily intake was 16 tablets, 8 tablets of Oxycontin and 8 of Soma. I made the decision to wean off the Soma first.

The thought was since the Soma was mainly a muscle relaxant with a bit of pain reliever in it, it would allow me to continue taking my big pain reliever, Oxycontin.

My withdrawal journey began on January 1st, 2010, and on August 1st, 2010, I had completely eliminated the Soma from my pain management regimen. At that point in time, I decided to take 3 months off before my next battle of eliminating Oxycontin. A break that was well deserved after the 7-month-long commitment it took to completely break the habit of Soma. A commitment that had moments of doubts, challenges, and much frustration for myself and, at times, for my family.

The decision for a break caused some concerns and issues for most of my loved ones. I believe they thought I would never have enough motivation again to endure what I had just gone through.

I assured them that I would be mentally prepared after the 3-month break by the beginning of November.

Without the benefit of taking Soma, my ability to be calm and relaxed enough to sleep at night was becoming very difficult and was more challenging as time went on.

Even though I hadn't taken any Soma for 3 months, I was still pounding down 8 Oxycontin a day and knew getting off these would be drastically more difficult.

Just the thought of minimally reducing my daily dose of Oxycontin filled me with anxiety and fear. I guess the fear was not being able to do it and failing both myself and my family.

Since the narcotic Oxycontin is so addictive, my pain management physician, Dr. Douglas, suggested reducing my Oxycontin intake by only half a tablet per month. He explained about the toxicity of Oxycontin and that I was obliviously addicted to them, at no fault of my own, due to the amount that I took and the length of time that I had been taking them, almost 9 years at this point. Dr. Douglas also warned me that reducing 1 whole tablet in my daily dose could be a severe risk to my health and even my life.

As it turned out, I learned there was no way for me to eliminate 1 whole tablet a month as I did with the Soma. I would have either gone crazy or died.

When November first arrived, I started the battle of eliminating Oxycontin. It had been 3 months since ending my dependency on Soma, and now came the battle for my life.

I approached getting off the Oxy the same as getting off the Soma. I had to decide when I should reduce just the half tablet of Oxycontin in the day. Since I was taking 8 Oxy a day and only cutting out one half of a tablet (which equated to 1/16 that I was previously taking), I didn't think it would be that difficult.

My feeling was, this won't be too bad; I'll still be taking 7 ½ of my original 8 tablets a day. That "not-too-bad" feeling didn't last long because my body and brain instantly realized I was short-changing it.

Boy, was I wrong!

After 16 months of hell eliminating Oxycontin, I found myself in somewhat of a predicament. I made a self-imposed deadline of being completely clean by January 1st, 2012.

As December approached, I felt like my withdrawal symptoms were becoming easier to tolerate, but I still had to wean off the last whole Oxy.

Continuing the same pattern for the Oxy withdrawal that I had been on for over a year now meant I would be completely drug-free by the end of January 2012.

I felt confident my goal was attainable continuing on this path, but I started to think how nice it would be to be drug-free by the end of 2011.

To achieve my goal by the end of 2011 meant I had to cut out the last whole Oxy by the end of the month, not a ½ as I had been doing for all the months up to this point. My dose in December would be my last Oxy forever and I mean forever!

With much thought and discussion with my family and with Dr. Douglas, I made the decision to go for it and made December 31st, 2011 my last day of opiate addiction. God help me.

My Journey Ends

As the end of December 2011 approached, reality was starting to hit me. This is it! I'm almost at the end of my 2-year journey to sobriety. I must say the month flew by because of the Christmas holidays and all the activities that came with it. As mentioned before, both Erica and Brad have birthdays in December, the 29th and the 30th, respectively.

Brad wanted to go snowboarding with his best friend, Matt, up at Big Bear Mountain for his birthday. Big Bear was about 150 miles from home, just about a 3-hour drive considering the winding road up the mountainside.

With Brad and Erica's birthday celebrations going on, Chris and I planned to take Brad and Matt snowboarding on December 31st, 2011, New Year's Eve.

Since the ski resorts are always very crowded over the New Year holiday, we wanted to make the most of the day for the boys. We drove up to the base of the mountain the night before and checked into a hotel. That way, we could get up very early the following day and head up the mountain so the boys could hit the slopes as early as possible.

After arriving at the ski resort and dropping off the boys, Chris and I left and went to explore the town of Big Bear. We had been to Big Bear so many times prior to this trip that there wasn't much left to explore. So that basically meant browsing around the many unique shops the area has to offer.

If you knew my wife, you would know the day couldn't start without a Starbucks coffee, which meant Starbucks would be one of the first stops of the day.

It was around 11:30 am when we arrived at Starbucks at the bottom of the ski resort where Brad and Matt were snowboarding. We went in, ordered our drinks, and took them back to our truck. In the back of my mind, I was thinking, this is my last day of taking any kind of opiate. The thought of taking my very last hit was really causing me anxiety.

Chris and I sat there and talked about anything and everything, including when I was going to take this last opiate.

As usual, I had wrapped up the Oxy in a piece of aluminum foil and had it in the coin pocket of my jeans. For some reason, I got the idea to take the Oxy out of my pocket and unwrap it, and as I sat there and looked at it, I reflected on my life as a drug addict and the pain I had inflicted on everyone. Then, without hesitation, I threw my last Oxy ever in my mouth and swallowed it. I guess I had done this routine so many times over the past 10 years that it was a natural reaction.

Bam! Just like that, it was over. I had just taken the last Oxycontin of my lifetime. No re-dos, no pulling it back out, no regurgitating it, no nothing. It was done, finished, over with!

Now, after nearly 10 years of addiction and 2 years of going through the withdrawal process, I was officially "Drug-Free"!

Actually, as big as the challenge was to wean off the drugs, I had a more significant challenge ahead of me, the challenge to stay drug-free. I knew this was going to be a lifelong struggle and a challenge that was going to be a roller coaster ride with many ups and down

Chapter 21: The Struggles After Kicking My Addiction

The human brain is extremely powerful, as I learned the hard way. At the start of my withdrawal process, my brain knew it wasn't getting the same amount of the drug as the month before. I didn't feel it so much with the Soma as with the Oxycontin.

Reducing the Soma was more of an inconvenience than anything else, not to say I didn't experience any withdrawal symptoms. Still, it definitely helped me prepare for the task of getting off the Oxycontin.

Just eliminating half of an Oxycontin a month was like nothing I had ever experienced before. You would think going from 8 Oxycontin a day to 7 ½ Oxycontin a day was no big deal, but holy shit, it was a huge deal! My brain was aware of the exact quantity of opiates my body was consuming every day, and any reduction in that quantity was noted.

With only that half of an Oxycontin tablet missing from my daily consumption, my brain sent out signals trying to locate the other half. The signals were sent to every nook and cranny in my body, giving me the feeling of flu-like symptoms, including body aches, nausea, fever, chills, headaches, body shakes, and so on.

An easy and instant remedy for these symptoms would be to take an Oxycontin, and all my pain and mental anguish would go away. Unfortunately, this remedy wasn't an option for me. I'm sure I would become immediately addicted again, and in a matter of no time, I would be back to taking 8 Oxycontin or more a day, just like I was during my addiction.

Now, after 10 years since December 31, 2011, the last day that I took any opiate, my brain still goes looking for the drugs that I fed it for 10 years. During the first year, after completely weaning off the drugs, I would experience these flu-like symptoms at least once a month, and they would last anywhere from a week to a few days. These flu-like symptoms were so bad that all I wanted to do was lay down, sleep, and ride it out until they passed.

As the years of sobriety have passed, these flu-like symptoms still return but with less frequency. In the last few years, these withdrawal flu-like symptoms that continue to haunt me only come 2 to 3 times a year and generally pass within 2 or 3 days. I've come to accept these periods of discomfort.

Not that I'm a veteran with these incidents, I know that I just must chill and get on with it. These occurrences are also a little reminder of how much I've achieved, and I never want to go back to that deep, dark place I was at for nearly 10 years.

I barely made it through all this, maintaining my marriage, my relationships with my kids and family, and my will to live. There's no way any of my loved ones will put up with me again if I return to using drugs. I can never let addiction happen to me again because I've already played all my "Mulligans" - golf term for a do-over - for this round of life, and there are no more to take.

Let me try to explain my feelings about the "pain management" regimen I was placed on for nearly 10 years. I still experience excruciating pain, and it tests my will every day.

The pain medicine I was being prescribed, like all pain meds, was just a nerve blocker, blocking the sense of pain going to the brain. The meds don't take the pain away; they just mask it.

Now that I'm no longer dependent on any kind of narcotics for pain relief, I've come to realize that this constant pain is never, ever going away. Sometimes, I have a tough time realizing this and feel sorry for myself. Oh, poor baby! I've always maintained that if an ordinary person were experiencing the pain that I have to endure every day, they would think their back was broken and would head to the hospital to seek treatment.

As we get older, our bodies start to diminish slowly year after year. Everyone is prone to this. It's nature's way of telling us that we're getting older. Unfortunately, the injury started my decline way too early in life for me.

I'm constantly reminded that I have a damaged spine with almost every movement I make. Bending over is now limited due to levels that are fused in my back. When I need to get something off the floor, I generally must squat like a girl to pick it up. When putting my shoes on, if I'm not able to lift my foot onto something like a bench or chair, I now must use a long shoehorn because of my limitations.

When I do any kind of activity, my back becomes so stiff that I can barely move within minutes of stopping. It is so painful to stretch or try to loosen it back up. The stiffness is probably the most painful issue that I deal with all the time, every day. I can genuinely say that I've accepted the condition of my back and the pain associated with it. I know now that the pain is never going away, and I'll have to deal with it for the rest of my life.

I honestly still consider myself fortunate; there are so many other health issues with more deadly consequences that I could have been dealt.

Chapter 22: My First Challenge

My own journey came with many trials and tribulations, but in the end, we are all in agreement the journey was worth it.

Within a year of becoming drug-free, I was faced with the first of many future challenges. I somehow experienced a ruptured tendon in my right forearm, and the pain was extreme. I went to the doctor for an examination and was told that the injury needed immediate surgery.

Apparently, after suffering a ruptured tendon, the tendon tends to want to attach to some other part of the bone other than its original and specific bone that it ruptured from.

Within a few days, I was having surgery, not a major one like my previous back surgeries, but still, a surgery that came with severe pain post-op. Considering I had been completely drug-free for only a few months, and the typical protocol for post-surgery pain relief was prescribing some sort of pain-reducing narcotic, this is where my dilemma began. I thought to myself, "How am I going to deal with the post-surgery pain without the benefit of any pain meds?".

While discussing my predicament with the doctor, she suggested that following the surgery, before stitching me back up and putting the cast on my arm, she would inject me with multiple doses of Lidocaine around the site of the surgery.

Lidocaine is a local, nonnarcotic anesthetic, or numbing medication, that stops the nerves from sending pain signals to the brain and reduces the pain and discomfort caused by an invasive medical procedure.

The surgery was completed at the outpatient pavilion at Sharp Memorial Hospital in San Diego, CA, and was a 2-hour procedure. Shortly after the surgery and waking up in the recovery room, I was discharged and returned home to finish my recovery. There's nothing like being at home and recovering compared to staying in the hospital. There is a major mental advantage to recovering at home.

The surgery was performed on a Thursday. The next day, on a Friday, Chris, Brad, Brad's friend Matt, and I headed over to Palm Desert to ring in the New Year at the Marriott, our favorite desert destination. I felt exceptionally well, considering my surgery was done the day before. That evening, we all walked over to the JW Marriott Hotel, where there was a massive New Year's Party going on.

To my surprise, I was somewhat pain-free, but I did have a good beer or two, possibly three, to help with any discomfort! I literally took only one extra strength Tylenol. Apparently, with the extra doses of Lidocaine the doctor had given me, the pain was kept to a minimum. Especially during the first few days after surgery when the pain level is generally elevated. Whatever it was, I survived the trip and enjoyed myself with minimal pain or discomfort.

Unfortunately, I've had to go through 5 surgeries since my drug sobriety, and each time, I've had to face the same challenge of dealing with post-surgery pain without the benefit of pain-reducing narcotics.

Before every surgery, while waiting in the pre-op area, a nurse conducted many different tests and evaluations, including EKG, temperature, pulse, and blood pressure, among others. These were necessary to make sure my health was acceptable for a safe surgery. She also prepped the area where the surgery was to be performed. During this time, I also had visits from both the surgeon and the anesthesiologist to introduce themselves and explain what they would be doing.

The anesthesiologist explained to me how I would be sedated. This is when I always took the opportunity to explain my past opiate addiction to them. I explained this to ensure they completely understood my situation, the fact that, under no circumstances could I have any form of opiate in my sedation cocktail.

Apparently, opioids are widely used for pre-anesthetic medication. Introducing any amount or any form of an opiate would be an absolute disaster for me and would have an irreversible effect.

It would be like giving an alcoholic a drink after they were sober for years or a cigarette to a person who had successfully quit smoking.

Speaking of smoking, I was a cigarette smoker for many years and finally decided to quit even though I really enjoyed it. I successfully quit smoking cigarettes and overcame my nicotine addiction in 1999. I knew if I had only one cigarette or even a drag off a cigarette that it would lead me to smoke again.

The health benefits from being a nonsmoker compared to the consequences your body suffers from smoking are overwhelming. It benefits your health and your wallet now that a pack of cigarettes costs $7 to $10. Also, the cigarette smoke just lingers on your clothes and makes your breath very unappealing.

I got my opportunity to quit when I was visiting my cousin Randy who lived in Las Vegas. Randy has always enjoyed going boating, so he decided to take us out on Lake Mead.

On this day, I was under the weather with a messed-up stomach, feeling really bad and nauseated. After making it through the day on the lake and returning to his house for the evening, I decided to go into his garage and attempt to smoke a cigarette. Bad decision!

I felt so sick after having the cigarette that it caused me to vomit throughout the night. This was the moment I decided to quit, and that was the last cigarette I ever smoked. The day was July 11, 1999, and I've been nicotine-free since that day, which is over 20 years now. Little did I know that the withdrawal symptoms that I experienced quitting cigarettes were minuscule compared to quitting narcotics.

There have been times when I'm stopped at a red light, and the person in the car in front of me is smoking. When they take a hit from their cigarette and exhale it, I catch the smell of the smoke. I kind of enjoy that, and to this day, I still love the smell of cigarette smoke.

It has been said that nicotine is as addicting as heroin, and they're the toughest addictions to quit successfully. My success in quitting cigarettes played a big part in my victory in kicking the opiate habit. Knowing I had quit cigarettes for roughly 12 years, and not really having to fight the temptation of smoking again, I knew I had the fight in me that the opiate withdrawal was going to take. I've had to accept and conquer the challenges of kicking two of the most addictive habits known to man in my lifetime.

When I ultimately ended my addiction to opiates on December 31, 2011, I knew it would be a daily struggle for the rest of my life. I knew this would be a day-to-day fight just like the nicotine fight had been, but I wasn't going to fail. I would not only be failing myself but failing everyone else who had supported me.

Chapter 23: If It Wasn't for Pot, I'd Be on Drugs©

I know most people consider marijuana, commonly called "pot" or "weed", to be a drug and a drug that can become addictive. Some even say that marijuana can be the gateway for a life of drug use. I know it sounds a bit hypocritical, but I've never considered pot to be more of a drug than alcohol.

I've always said I would rather get into a car with someone who's been smoking a little pot than a person who's been drinking alcohol.

Growing up in Southern California, pot was always around and very accessible. Back in my youth, you could buy a bag of weed for $10.

Back then, a bag of weed was also called a "lid." It would come in a regular sandwich tuck and flip baggie without a zip lock. Back then, the "Ziplock bag" hadn't been invented!

The quantity of pot in these lids was an eyeball measurement using your fingers. The pot would be placed into the baggie, and you would put your 4 fingers horizontally to the bag. When the quantity of the pot in the baggie would get to the height of the 4 fingers, it would be considered a lid. I don't recall these baggies of pot ever being measured by the weight.

Most of the pot back in the 70s came from Mexico, and it wasn't very pretty to look at compared to what's being produced today. Even after it was placed in baggies for sale, it still came with lots of stems, seeds, and sometimes other stuff such as tiny rocks from the harvesting. Some of the more expensive and higher-end grades of pot back then were Columbian, Thai Sticks, and Panama Red, still coming to the United States by way of Mexico.

Over the decades, the quality and strength of marijuana has continued to improve. There are now different strains with different potencies, even different strains for various medical conditions.

The art of growing marijuana has brought on a whole new industry now that many of the states have legalized pot for either recreational or medical purposes.

As more and more people are getting educated on the benefits of marijuana, acceptance of marijuana is gaining. When it comes to using it for medical purposes, I'm a big believer that the benefits totally outweigh any conceivable cons that marijuana use would have.

Twelve years ago, when I started my road to sobriety, the choices for using pot were limited. You either smoked it in a joint, a pipe, or a bong. You could ingest by adding it to brownies so you could eat it instead of smoking it. Another option was to make a tea, boiling the leave and stems.

Now with the popularity of marijuana on the rise, the marijuana industry has invented new ways to deliver it to the body.

There are new edibles such as baked goods, cookies, muffins, etc.

There are even gummies that are eaten just like candy gummies.

Vape cartridges use battery-charged pens to heat the marijuana oil, and then you inhale it. They even make drops you can put on your tongue.

All these marijuana products come in all the different strains, depending on what your need is.

These products either come in the THC or the CBD versions.

Let me quickly explain the differences:

THC is known for giving the person a "high." It's generally recommended to people who want to take their mind off their pain while also experiencing relief.

CBD is recommended for those whose pain is primarily caused by inflammation and those who want to continue their day with regular mental function.

So many people of different ages used to have a negative opinion of marijuana, many of whom suffer from some kind of chronic, debilitating physical or mental health issue that will last the rest of their lives. Most likely, they've been prescribed some sort of medication. A lot of times, these prescriptions require taking a combination of more than one type of medication daily.

Now that marijuana is becoming more acceptable in society, more people suffering from illness or disease are turning to it. They realize the effects of marijuana are far less detrimental to your health and well-being than "big pharma."

Medical marijuana is an increasingly popular alternative to traditional pain-relieving medications, including opioids. Marijuana may ease certain types of chronic pain, including pain resulting from nerve damage and inflammation.

People who suffer from eating or sleeping disorders, anxiety, and all sorts of other health issues are trying it and realizing the benefits of pot. More people suffer from chronic pain than cancer, heart disease, and diabetes combined.

I understand this approach of dabbling in marijuana isn't for everyone, but it benefitted me. When it was time for me to start the course of getting off the prescribed narcotics, pot was a true blessing. A blessing that has assisted me in staying away from narcotics for 10 years.

Some people will read this book and probably think this behavior is absurd, a way of trading one drug for another. Again, I have never considered marijuana to be a drug that you should be punished for.

Some people are convinced that pot is a gateway drug that leads to other hard-core street drugs, and I'll never be convinced of that either. In my opinion, street drugs are crack, meth, heroin, etc., but never marijuana.

For me, I took a pain management cocktail of Oxycontin and Soma for years, and it only led to the decay of my mind and body. It's that old saying, "the cure is sometimes worse than the disease." I know for a fact this can be true. Marijuana definitely helped me with the nausea and the anxiety that I experienced when I went through 2 years of withdrawals.

This is my opinion and I'm entitled to it!

Chapter 24: I Don't Want to Play

As I've mentioned before, my family is very close, and we're together very often. Over time, at family get-togethers, I became more and more unwilling to participate in any of the fun. I would pretty much show up and find somewhere to plant my ass.

As a family gathering would continue through the day and into the evening, I would attempt to join in. My attempts most of the time were half-hearted, and I knew everyone there felt my minimal efforts.

As I carried on through my years of drug addiction, my lack of enthusiasm started to affect practically every aspect of my life. I lost pretty much any desire to go anywhere and do any activity. I would rather sit at home and wait for the time to take my next narcotic cocktail.

My behavior was affecting not only me but everyone around me. I was quite aware of this, even when I would try to put forward my best effort.

There was never any lack of effort by my loved ones and friends when it came to trying to spend time with me. I could tell that sometimes, they had difficulty trying to find something to talk about, considering my situation with my injury and the drugs. I was no longer the fun and smart-ass person I used to be.

Before my injury, I would consider myself a social butterfly and very outgoing. I was always the first to accept a challenge and never short of things to talk about. One of my greatest qualities was the ability to speak to anyone. At gatherings and parties, I used to be the first one

to join in and would make the most fun possible. I would joke and poke fun at people, which I expected to do.

When the family gatherings were planned, I knew it was going to be a fun-filled day. I used to really look forward to seeing all my family and playing around with my kids, nieces, cousins, and their kids.

Watching all the kids swimming in the pool would remind me of how my cousins and I did the same growing up: I was fortunate enough that my Aunt Gerry and Uncle Clyde had a pool. They lived directly across the street from me for my entire childhood. At that time, my aunt and uncle were one of the few who had a pool, and it was pretty much open to the neighborhood; and the neighborhood took advantage of their kindness.

Due to the severity and the repercussions from my injury, my interest and enthusiasm to participate like I once did were turned upside down.

I knew, and I think everyone knew by then, that I was just existing and not actually living. Now that I can look back and reflect on how pitiful my life had become, I can genuinely say I now understand how every day of being alive is a gift. It's a gift that shouldn't be taken for granted, and tomorrow is no guarantee. I should have learned this from my mother's shortened life due to cancer, but obviously, I didn't until I had to come to grips with my own struggles.

When my family got together for a birthday, graduation, anniversary, holiday, etc., rarely would anyone from the family not be in attendance to enjoy the celebration of the moment. There was always some sort of meal being served with massive amounts of food.

The family would always play games after eating. It was generally a game or two of "Left, Right, Center." This is a group game where you can be eliminated and then be brought back into the game with a roll of the dice. It's a great game to play with lots of people because it doesn't take a lot of smarts or concentration, and all the separate conversations can continue.

Erica and Brad would make a secret partnership in most of these games. If either one of them won the money prize, they would split the winnings between them. The ante for each game would be $3 per person, so it was common for the pot to be $60 or more. This little partnership increased their odds of winning. Their thinking was, winning something is better than not winning anything at all!

Since getting off the drugs, I've found that my enthusiasm and willingness to be back in the mix at family gatherings and other functions has returned.

Chapter 25: The Move to Florida

The move from San Diego to Florida in July 2014 was probably the most significant decision I had to make in my entire life, as I have a large family, and we've always been extremely close.

During this time, one concern that was always on my mind was the fact that I had only been off the narcotics for a little over 2 years. I knew this was going to be tough on me mentally, not only because of the move but also leaving the support I had from my extended family in San Diego. Even after 2 years of being sober, I had to continually fight the demons of addiction and was still experiencing withdrawal symptoms fairly frequently.

Once I was drug-free and realized how lucky I was to be still alive, I felt like I needed a change in environment. I thought about how Chris had moved around a few times in her lifetime, so why not give it a try?

Chris moved to New Jersey from England as a kid when her father was transferred to the United States. She had also moved to a few different locations in England and several towns in the greater London area. Ultimately, she made the major move across the pond to San Diego to share her life with me.

I also thought that if I had lived in San Diego my whole life without experiencing living in a different city, I would be a sad soul.

After about 10 years of Chris living in America, her parents, Peter and Pam, decided to emigrate to the United States. Chris's sister Vivienne also lived in San Diego at the time and was only a few minutes away from us. Their move to Southern California meant they would be near both of their daughters, something they had missed for quite a few years.

Her parents adapted easily to the American way of life. I remember her father always insisted on wearing a dress shirt, a tie, and a jacket when he would go out most of the time. It could be for dinner or running to the grocery store, and he would want to wear a jacket or at the very least a tie. It didn't take him long before he became accustomed the SoCal ways. He started wearing short sleeve shirts, shorts, and either tennis shoes or sandals.

For Chris's mother Pam, she immediately fitted into her new lifestyle. She purchased a new red 2003 Volkswagen Jetta and still has the same car today! The funny thing about her car is that after more than 18 years of owning that Volkswagen Jetta, the car only has around 11,000 miles. A real grandmother's car!

Once her parents made the move, they were always included in my family get-togethers and were immediately welcomed and became very comfortable hanging out with everyone.

I must say, my family is extremely difficult to be around and socialize with. **Just kidding**, nothing can be further from the truth. My family is another true blessing.

When Chris and I made the decision to move to Florida, her parents decided to move with us.

Their decision was based on a few reasons. One of those was the fact that Vivienne, Chris's sister, moved to Chapel Hill, North Carolina, only a few years after they came to America.

With their decision, we now had the task of trying to find 2 new homes in Florida, both having pretty much the same criteria. This made the search process much more difficult.

Chris and I traveled to Florida frequently, going at least 3 times a year for over 2 years, searching for 2 new homes without finding any desirable houses. Before each trip, we would do endless research, planning which housing projects we might possibly be interested in looking at, along with the different cities and towns.

On one of our trips, we went to a new development to see what kind of homes were being built and the area surrounding the development. As we entered the models, we were greeted by a salesperson named David.

Unfortunately for us, his development didn't have any inventory of the lots we were interested in. David suggested some other developments his company was building that might be of interest to us, now that he knew what we were looking for. We explored all of them, still without having any luck. David was restricted in helping us view other new housing developments since he was representing this builder and was contractually limited to only this developer's projects.

At the end of that trip, we returned to San Diego and had our doubts about ever finding new homes in Florida. At this point, Chris and I had made around 7 or 8 unsuccessful trips to Florida.

I knew that our unsuccessful house-hunting trips to Florida were met with much pleasure from my family and friends who never wanted us to leave.

After much discussion and soul searching, we began to wonder if our plans for Florida were in vain. Chris and I decided to make one last trip to Florida in the hopes of relocating.

We reached out to David and asked if he knew of a seasoned real estate agent who knew the area and style of home we were interested in and who could assist us in our search. David had a professional business relationship with a real estate agent named Carla, whom he introduced to us via phone.

Once we booked and made plans for our trip, we talked to Carla to confirm our requirements. Carla then did her research and sent us anything she thought might be of interest. A list of properties was compiled, so we were ready to go and view the homes on the list as soon as we arrived in Florida.

I knew my sister, Vicki, the kids, my father, and many others were praying to God that we would have another unsuccessful trip. It was known to all of them that this was our final trip, and if we returned to San Diego this time empty-handed, Florida was out of our plans.

There have only been a few members of my family who have ever left San Diego, and I would be the first one out of my immediate family.

The last and final trip was only scheduled for a few days, and it was going to be intense viewing all the homes on our list. Some of the requirements of our new homes were: preferably new with either a lake or a golf course view; absolutely no other home behind us; a three-car garage; a backyard facing West. We were adamant about the backyard facing West. We both wanted to see the beautiful sunsets just like we had in San Diego.

Upon arriving in Florida late one evening in November 2013, we met with Carla in person for the first time in our hotel lobby. We sat down to discuss the order of homes we were going to view and the strategy for the next 2 days. Once the viewing order was figured out, we hit the road and didn't stop.

In our previous trips to Florida, we would frequently come to a new development only to strikeout. Maybe the start time for a new phase of the development would be unknown. Sometimes there would be a sign stating the entire development was "Coming Soon," with no date for when it would be released.

On the second day of viewing with Carla, we came to a development, Johns Lake Pointe, in the City of Winter Garden, that was opening for sales in a few weeks. Surprisingly, it was one of the developments Chris and I had viewed on an earlier visit to Florida, but the development had been one of those with a "Coming Soon" sign.

Apparently, Carla had spoken to the real estate agent, Michael, prior to our arrival. Michael was the one who was going to oversee sales for this community. She planned for us to view the models that were built and furnished, even though the development wouldn't be officially open for sales for a few more weeks. Michael understood our situation of being out-of-towners and that our time was very limited.

The Johns Lake Pointe property was the first one we were going to look at for the day. As it turned out, it would be the only property we would visit.

Once we arrived, we were greeted by Michael, and he gave us the sales pitch about the property and invited us to go and view the models. The sales center was in the garage of one of the models. It had been transformed to give the appearance of a proper sales center.

To view the model that housed the sales center, you were required to exit the sales center and enter the model through the front door. Chris and I thought this particular model would be a good fit for her parents, and the larger model next door would be a good fit for us.

Finally, we had found a development that had potential.

Once we walked through the front door of the model, the home we thought would be suitable for her parents, I turned and looked at Chris smiling. I leaned in and whispered in her ear, "I want this home." The entrance of the home was very impressive, with an open floor plan with 11-foot ceilings. Pretty stunning, I must say.

Trying to hide our enthusiasm that we may have finally found something with potential, we continued the tour of the models. We returned to the sales center and met with Michael.

We sat down at his desk, and he asked what we thought. We expressed that we may be interested and asked what other information he could provide us with. Michael provided us with the limited marketing materials he had at this point and discussed what the standard options were and what items could be upgraded.

I think Michael included a lot of the upgraded items that were in the model that weren't really standard, but he said they were. He made a very tempting proposition.

He offered us the opportunity to go and look at the lots that would be available in the first phase of construction. Much to our surprise, the first lots released in phase one were the best backing onto the lake in this community of 51 future homes.

There were only 4 lots being released for purchase at that time. Chris and I went to walk the 4 lots and realized the lots had everything on our checklist. Nice large, wide, deep lots, right on Johns Lake, with the backyard facing directly West. Perfect! Perfect! Perfect!

We went back to the Sales Center and spoke again with Michael expressing some interest, but not being overzealous. We said we would return to the hotel to discuss our thoughts and get back to him the next morning.

We went back to the hotel and gave Chris's parents a call, saying we might have found our future new homes. They really needed to get to Florida asap, so they could take a firsthand look before any final decision was made.

Chris's father frantically made flight arrangements and they were in Florida the very next afternoon. That afternoon, all of us went back to the development so her parents could have a look at the models, lot location, and the surrounding area.

When we arrived at the sales center, Michael greeted us and was introduced to Peter and Pam. We shared with Michael that not only were Chris and I were possibly interested, but her parents were too. You could tell he was trying to contain himself at the thought of possibly getting two houses under contract before the development had officially opened!

My thinking was we have some serious leverage on any negotiations prior to presenting any others. As it turned out, Michael did in fact go overboard on what he was offering as far as upgrades at no cost.

When Chris and I and her parents returned to our hotel that evening, we had lots to talk about. Our decision was going to be a life-altering decision that could last a lifetime.

We decided we would put an offer in for a home like the model that housed the Sales Center. Peter and Pam decided on the same model as we did on a lot just up the street.

Carla planned to meet with all of us early the next morning before we flew back to San Diego so we could finalize the purchases and give the initial deposit that was required.

After completing our purchase agreement, I went for a walk by myself. I wanted some time to absorb what we had just done. The reality of buying a new home and relocating to Florida was a bit surreal. Chris stayed behind to assist her parents with their contract for their new house.

My walk took me to the lake located at the end of the street where my new house was to be built. There was a viewpoint that captured the entire lake. While I was there, my feelings and emotions were all over the place. After 3 years of coming down to Florida to look for a new home, it had finally all come together.

I also had immediate feelings of guilt, knowing I'd soon be leaving all my loved ones in California. I could no longer go and see them anytime I wanted to and would miss all the family birthdays and other celebrations.

Both of our new homes were going to take some time to be built, approximately 6 to 7 months until completion around the end of July 2014. This time frame left about 6 months for my family to adjust to the idea of us moving, which made it a little easier to accept.

As it turned out, in the more than 7 years of living in Florida, we make it back to San Diego pretty frequently. Almost every 3 months or less, I travel out there to visit. The time between my visits seems to go by very quickly.

I must say, now when we go back to San Diego to visit, we spend more quality time with family and it's a lot more meaningful.

Chapter 26: A Letter from My Sister Vicki

Dear Greg,

First let me tell how grateful I am for you taking the courageous step and fighting the fight of your life with the battle of pain medication addiction. You asked for honesty, and the truth is I was very scared of what was happening to you and what could happen to you in addition to the impact it was having on your loved ones.

At the time I was at a loss of what to do to help you and when it came to the point of considering an intervention, I thanked God, you took it upon yourself to take action and get out of this hell hole you were going through.

I personally was so worried I was going to lose the only sibling I have in life, and it was more than I could bear on my own, so I continued to pray for an answer.

Writing this, I am honestly in tears reflecting on this period of time. While I could never understand or know the pain you were in, I know I had a hard time dealing with the abrupt changes in your mood. It wasn't my brother and I just wanted you back the way it was before your surgeries and addiction. I struggled with knowing what to do to help you, Chris, your children, Dad, and the rest of the family. I know we tried to keep Dad from knowing about some of the not so pleasant episodes. He went through so much with Mom, and it was hard to see his son in pain, and he shared with me he felt hopeless in knowing what to do for you.

I would hold my breath at times answering a call from Chris, scared there was an issue or something even worse. I have to say, there were times of embarrassment when something would set you off and it would be witnessed in front of friends or in public view. I knew this wasn't you but the drugs, but it still wasn't easy to experience.

I am so thankful to God you fought this addiction, stayed focus, and endured the time it took. You have shared that you know the effects it had on you, and I am proud of the path you took and continue to take to remain free of these drugs.

I have learned a lot from your experience, and I truly believe it can be inspirational to others.

Love you with all my heart,

Your Sister,

Vicki

What can I say about my sister and my brother-in-law David? Both Vicki and David have always been there for me at every point
in my life, in good times and in bad times. They've also tried to be there for everyone they know, especially when it comes to their family.

Their commitment is unwavering and has always been non-judgmental, and that alone had to be a challenge when it came to dealing with me.

Ever since my mother's passing, my sister has tried to be the family matriarch, and I mean that in only the best of terms. Her commitment to keeping both our immediate and extended family close together, especially on holidays, has been a blessing.

As a child, my aunts, uncles, and cousins were always together on holidays and for special events, and those moments are great memories and have a special place in my heart. My sister has been steadfast in keeping these traditions going so the next generation will realize the importance of family being together on these special days.

Vicki and David's house has always had an open-door policy, no matter if you're family or not.

Even my children's friends have experienced Vicki and Dave's hospitality. They have always been welcomed and invited for dinner, a party, or even a place to stay the night when needed.

When Chris and I moved to Florida, Brad was just starting college at Sonoma State University, some 500 miles away from San Diego. Whenever he had a break from school, he would always return to San Diego.

At the time, neither Chris, myself, nor Brad really had a plan for where he would spend his days and nights while he was on break.

Vicki and David took it upon themselves, without being asked, to have him stay with them. They would feed and house him, never once asking him for money to help with expenses.

While he was there, I know they checked with him every day to see if he was going to be there for dinner or maybe ask what his plans for the day might be. I think they enjoyed having him around!

As Brad's parents, we had the luxury of never really having to worry if he was okay because Vicki and David were always there for him. **This was a great relief.**

Vicki and David have also always been the second set of parents to our other 2 children, Brett and Erica. They were always there to help with anything they needed, including supporting them in their sports and school activities when they were younger. Even now that my kids are adults, they continue to support them unconditionally, no questions asked.

The care and support Vicki and David also provide for my father is incredible. They live 5 minutes away from his house and are constantly running errands for him. These errands include picking up groceries for him, taking him to his doctor appointments, and either making him dinner or picking a dinner up for him. Ninety percent of the time, they provide a home-cooked meal for him, and it's always something fresh and healthy. I can honestly say I don't how they do it, considering how full their plates are all the time.

Vicki and David already have three grandchildren. Two boys and a girl from their daughter Amber and her husband, Adam. A fourth grandchild is on the way from their other daughter Ashley and her husband Kevin, and their baby girl will have arrived by the time this book is published.

Amber and her children live up in Huntington Beach, about 100 miles from them, but they go up there to see them at every possible opportunity.

What I've told you about Vicki and David and the support they give to everyone is just the tip of the iceberg. I'm truly blessed to have a sister like Vicki and a brother-in-law like David. They both played a significant role in my survival and path to sobriety.

I love you Vicki and David so much, and words cannot express my gratitude and appreciation for the support you both provided to me, and I'm sure it will continue.

Chapter 27: My Faith and My Church

My father was greatly concerned that my condition was putting my marriage at risk and took it upon himself to find me a new church.

I was brought up going to Christ the King Lutheran Church during my youth until transferring to Ascension Lutheran. I must admit there was a period in my life when I didn't attend church as much as I should have. I guess you can say, I kind of lost my way.

My father was successful in locating a Missouri Synod Lutheran church not far from my house, Mt. Olive Lutheran Church, and I worshipped there for 8 years up until my move to Florida.

Getting back into the church and worshipping God greatly improved me mentally, but I still felt like I was drowning. Taking one step forward and then falling two steps back. Even though I was getting healthier, the "pain management" drug cocktail was bringing me down, and I wasn't the person I once was.

Since I'm talking about my history of attending church, let me update you: When I moved from San Diego to Winter Garden, Florida, in July 2014, I went on a mission to find a new house of worship. A church just outside of our community was an option. Nothing wrong with it, but it was a nondenominational Christian church, and I really wanted a Missouri Synod Lutheran church.

After several months of searching, I was out running some errands, driving down a road when I noticed a church, Zion Lutheran Church. I had never noticed this church before, even though I had traveled down this road and passed it probably at least 100 times.

I pulled into the parking lot and went to the church's front door. The church secretary greeted me and opened the door to let me in. I explained to her that I had recently moved into the area and was looking for a new house of worship. She mentioned that the pastor might be available to speak to me if I would like to chat. I said sure and was soon introduced to a very young man.

To me, he looked like he was about the same age as my son, Brett. He reached out his hand to shake mine and introduced himself as Pastor Rojas. We went into his office, and we spoke for quite a while, learning about each other. It turned out that Pastor Rojas had just been ordained the previous year, and Zion was his first church to be the pastor.

Pastor Rojas is the spiritual leader I've never had before. His passion for the Lord's work goes without saying. His enthusiasm during the sermons, the lessons, and the gospel readings are invigorating, and he definitely keeps your attention. Some of my former pastors delivered their sermons in a very monotone voice, making it sometimes difficult to follow along or stay interested. This is never the case with Pastor Rojas.

I think Pastor Rojas was all of 26 years old when we first met. The problem with Pastor Rojas is the fact that he is so good that it makes him a great candidate for other churches in need of a new pastor. He's in such demand that it seems like he receives a calling to go to a new church once or twice a year. At the moment, though, he's entirely committed to his congregation at Zion.

Since I've been attending Zion for over 7 years and have had Pastor Rojas as my shepherd, my faith has only gotten stronger. Having such a strong faith has provided me with the courage to continue to be drug-free. I believe it has also helped me rebuild my relationships with most everyone back to where they were before my addiction.

Thanks be to God.

Chapter 28: My Surgeries in Florida

Since the move to Florida, my physical health has taken a beating. This has required me to go under the knife 4 more times.

Within 2 years of the move, my knees started causing me great pain and greatly limiting my ability to walk and stand.

For all the following surgeries, I had to go without the advantage of narcotics in my anesthesia or being prescribed any pain reliever other than Tylenol or Advil for the post-surgery pain.

Surgery #1: Left Knee Arthroscopy

I finally had no choice but to go to the doctor and see what could be done to get me back on track. I scheduled an appointment with Dr. Travis, an orthopedic surgeon, and went to visit him.

He seemed to have a good idea of what was causing my pain and felt confident he could ease most of, if not all, the current pain I was experiencing.

Dr. Travis suggested I have some X-rays and an MRI done to determine the precise cause of my discomfort and pain. Unfortunately, with me having an electronic spinal stimulator implanted into my back, MRIs are not an option for me.

The risk for me having an MRI is that this magnetic process could pull on the electric leads that are implanted in my back, causing them to be damaged or displaced or causing me excruciating pain.

Without the benefit of an MRI, the doctor really didn't have the information he needed to perform a successful surgery. Basically, the doctor would be going into the surgery "blind," having to explore, fix, and correct any damage to the joint. This surgery was an arthroscopic surgery.

Arthroscopy is a surgical procedure in which orthopedic surgeons uses a scope to visualize, diagnose, and treat problems inside a joint. These procedures are minimally invasive and generally have a quick recovery time for the patient.

During my consultation with Dr. Travis, I explained my past opioid addiction and made sure he understood the need to keep any form of opiate from entering my body. The fact is that even the smallest amount of an opiate injected into my body at this stage could ultimately lead to dependency and addiction again.

Chris drove me to the hospital when the day came for my exploratory knee surgery. After arriving and getting registered, I was escorted to the pre-surgery area to get prepped for my surgery.

Both Dr. Travis and the anesthesiologist came into my pre-op area to discuss the procedures that they were going to perform and asked if I had any questions or concerns. I took this opportunity to state again how important it was to respect my concerns about my anesthesia.

I reiterated, "Under no circumstances, NO opiate additives in my anesthetic sedation." Trust me; it was entirely understood by all involved with the surgery at this point. NO OPIATES!

With no other option for pain relief and to reduce the post-surgery pain, the Doctor injected a large quantity of Lidocaine in my knee.

During my post-surgery follow-up appointment, Dr. Travis said my knee was severely damaged, and the only remedy would require a knee replacement to get back to normal. He also said he was able to go into the knee joint and clean up the scar tissue and bone spurs that were accessible.

The pain experienced after arthroscopic surgery is nothing like the pain associated with invasive surgery, but it's still intense.

The cleaning up of the knee surgery afforded me almost a year of pain relief until it returned with a vengeance. Then the knee replacement surgery was scheduled, and the doctor decided I was a perfect candidate for robotic knee replacement.

Surgery #2: Left Knee Replacement

I needed to go to a digital imaging facility and have a specialized scan performed to have the robotic surgery. During this scan, a digital program was written onto a disk to direct the robot during the surgery. Once the scan was completed and the program was written, all that was left was for me to show up for the scheduled surgery.

I was told that the pain after knee replacement surgery would be more intense than the arthroscopic, along with a longer time for recovery.

I again discussed the form of anesthesia that was going to be used and insisted again that NO opiate additives be in my anesthesia sedation.

I also asked the doctor to inject my surgery area with lots of Lidocaine as he had previously done so I could get over the pain hurdle. The Lidocaine worked its magic and limited the pain level for almost 3 days. Unfortunately, after day 3, the pain really started to increase.

I've always had an issue with the after-effects of anesthesia, having been under sedation for several hours. It makes me nauseous for days and sometimes weeks. The nausea and the pain aren't a good combination for someone who has limited options for medication.

Another strange thing that happened after each surgery was I would completely lose my appetite for any kind of meat, primarily beef. I don't really know why this was, but it happened every time.

Once I started to regain my appetite for meat, I always started with ground beef first, never steak. Not a problem because I sure love my homemade tacos!

Surgery #3: Right Knee Arthroscopy

About a year and a half after the left knee replacement, my right knee started to feel like the left one did prior to getting it replaced. So off I went to visit my favorite, Dr. Travis, to have it checked out.

During the examination, my symptoms were similar to the ones I had with the left knee, so it was decided that I should have another exploratory surgery.

Dr. Travis went into the knee arthroscopically and cleaned out the knee joint of all scar tissue and bone spurs. He then made any repairs that were possible at the time and gave the whole knee joint a thorough internal inspection.

Once again, this procedure was performed without the benefit of any narcotic cocktail in the anesthesia or for the post-surgery pain.

Talking with the doctor about the surgery, he said that he had cleaned up the knee as best he could, that there was a lot of wear and tear on the knee, and that it would eventually need replacing. That was over 2 years ago, and the knee seems to be hanging in there with only occasional discomfort. Fingers crossed!

Surgery #4: Left Wrist Surgery

In the summer of 2019, I was in San Diego painting my father's house along with my cousin Randy.

I was standing on the third step of a ladder when I realized I needed to get some more paint. I turned around, completely forgetting I was on the ladder, and took a step back as if I were standing on the ground!

Realizing I was about to do a head-plant onto the concrete path, I made a quick effort to do a tuck and roll kind of motion, and instinctively I put my hand forward to break my fall.

After bouncing off the concrete, I expected to be bruised and bleeding, but at that moment, I only felt some wrist pain and continued with the painting. As the day went on, my wrist began to really hurt.

Once the house painting was completed, and my time to visit all my family and friends ended, I returned to Florida. As my life went on, the pain in my wrist also went on and wouldn't go away.

I was referred to Dr. Alan, who specialized in the hand and wrist. He wanted an MRI of my wrist, and, once again, an MRI wasn't an option. The surgery was scheduled, and Dr. Alan had to rely only on the X-rays that were taken.

This procedure was also considered an exploratory surgery since there wasn't an MRI to provide the extent of the injury, and the doctor went into the hand and wrist arthroscopically.

During the procedure, he searched to see the cause of the pain and fix whatever was possible. It was kind of the same game plan as it had been with Dr. Travis for my first knee surgery.

When I was getting prepped in the pre-op area, Dr. Alan checked in with me and ensured I was good and ready for the surgery.

When the anesthesiologist came in to have his little talk, I told him that I could NOT have any form of opioid in my anesthesia sedation. I explained to him about my past opiate addiction and my goal to remain drug-free.

He immediately became agitated with me, and his demeanor completely changed. His response was, "What do you want me to give you then?" and my reply was, "You're the doctor, not me; figure it out."

The nurse who was nearby at the time, getting me prepared for my surgery, heard the entire conversation. We both looked at each other and were amazed by what the anesthesiologist had just said. It wasn't only what he said but also the way he had said it.

The anesthesiologist left the area and went straight over to the nurse's station, where Dr. Alan was reviewing some charts and the nurse and I observed him discussing my "outrageous" request.

The nurse said to me, "Good for you for getting off the drugs. The anesthesiologist is an ass." Once Dr. Alan and the asshole anesthesiologist finished their chat, my doctor came back into my room and said, "It's all worked out; he didn't completely understand your situation and your past drug dependency."

The surgery was performed again without the benefit of a narcotic in my anesthesia or any narcotics for the pain. The surgery was successful, and the pain did eventually go away, but it took some time, over a year, to heal.

Chapter 29: A Letter from My Youngest Son Bradley

Hello, my name is Brad, and I am the youngest of my siblings and have spent most of my life seeing the ups and downs, trials, and tribulations of my dad. When my dad first told me that he was writing a book about his struggles and eventual triumph, I was so happy to hear he was in the right place emotionally, mentally, and physically to understand that who he was in the past wasn't the real Greg or our dad. It takes a great deal of maturity and strength to be willing to hear the impact he had on those around him, for good or bad. With this being said, before jumping into my memories and perspective, I want to say that my dad is my hero and truly is an inspiration by the way he has looked addiction, temptation, and evil straight in the eyes and said, "No more. Not today. Never Again." My intention for this piece is in no way to belittle, demean, or make fun of my dad. Rather it's to show and depict the progression and accomplishments that have brought my dad back to someone I'm comfortable and genuinely enjoy spending time with.

Additionally, I want to acknowledge the backbone and the number one supporter who made my father's recovery possible: my mom. As I began to think about particular experiences and memories relating to my dad, all of the emotions that came back to me were how my mom was treated, what she went through, and how she never gave up, even after all she was having to deal with. Without a doubt, my mom took the brunt of all that my dad was dishing out, yet she never gave up. Were there times when she vocalized that the two of them may need a break? Sure. But did they? No. This speaks volumes to the character, the values, the love, and, most importantly, the commitment that my mom upholds. I admire her truly for her strength and willingness to never give up or take the easy way out. They both stuck it out together and came out on the other side, still holding hands.

Taking Away My Teammate

Looking back on my early childhood, there are some distinctive memories of the fun and enjoyment I had with my dad. Back in the day, my dad would always have an evening smoke, and I vividly remember going out and throwing the ball with him while he enjoyed his cigarette. It was simple yet enjoyable. Just me and him tossing the ball back and forth, no talking, just a common bond, and enjoyment for sports. He was the one who sparked my passion for all things sports. From soccer to basketball to baseball to golf, he constantly encouraged me and actively played with me. With this being said, when my dad had his first major back injury, it was the start of the end for many years of my athletic dad participating and sharing in sports activities with me. For me, this was a major hit and the start of a slight disconnect between my dad and me. What once was a strong bond focused around playing sports together was now taken away. Without a doubt, I could ask him to play, and I could always rely on him to be willing to throw the ball or shoot some hoops. However, when the question was now asked to play, it was "Sorry bud, not today" or "I can't" or "My back is killing me, maybe tomorrow." This became the new norm, and just like that, I lost my teammate.

This theme would continue for many years, but occasionally, that one day would come when he would answer, "Yes. Let's go throw the ball." It was the highlight of my day. It finally is happening. My dad and I were getting back to our good old days of tossing ball in the evening, just him and me. However, it wasn't the same. The energy and encouragement that came from those moments early in my life had switched to tension and anxiety. If I didn't hit my dad perfectly in the chest with my throw, or it was a little wild, he wouldn't be able to grab it and would get angry and irritated. He would say, "Well, go grab it" or "I can't get those; you got to throw it better." At this point, I would be trying too hard to perfectly aim my throw, so I would leave it short or overthink it, resulting in me chasing the ball and seeing the dissatisfaction on his face. These "special moments" would only last 10-15 minutes before he was done throwing with me and went back inside. At this point, I had lost my teammate, my captain, and mentor. I'm sure my dad would have wanted nothing more than to play with me, but his physical limitations wouldn't allow it, and, as a result, that created anger, which was inevitably taken out on me. This was my earliest realization that my dad, after his back injury, wasn't the same man I knew before.

From Physical to Mental

As my dad began to have increased pain and stronger medications, the anger and mood swings became more aggressive and frequent. It made it difficult to have a conversation with my dad or, worse, ask permission to do something because you never knew what response or reaction you were going to get. It made me timid and hesitant to even want to talk to him. It wasn't like this all the time, but for most conversations, he had a tone of anger or irritation in his voice. On top of that, you just never knew what was what going to set him off, and that made me nervous to do really anything around him. If you did something wrong, even something that was minute, and he saw or heard it, there was going to be an altercation.

Some specific examples have stayed with me for some reason to this day. One occurred in 7th grade when I was riding my skateboard up our path to our front door, ran into the little step, and chipped a tile. My dad saw me trying to sneakily put the piece back and came out, yelling at me, asking what I was thinking, why would I ride my skateboard, and much more. He was heated, and to top it off, he said it in front of a girl I really liked at the time. I think that's why it stuck to me for so many years because my dad had no situational awareness or care for those around him. He was so enraged and focused on coming after me that he was blind to the surrounding environment.

Another time, we were simply in line waiting to get gas when a truck pulled up and took the pump we had been waiting for. Without hesitation, my dad got out of the car and charged at the driver, cussing him out and getting in his face. The driver of the truck deescalated the situation and simply apologized, saying he didn't know we were waiting. By the time this was resolved, the whole gas station was staring in utter disbelief that this man was causing such a scene over a silly gas pump. This is just a prime example of events that would or could happen every time we went out with my dad. No matter the person, environment, or situation, if something irritated him, you were going to know about it.

He had built this mindset that everyone and everything was out to get him. If something so minor went wrong or didn't go his way, he thought it was out to get him, and that would immediately change his mood, and he would just spiral down an emotional rabbit hole. He would get so low emotionally and let some small discrepancy ruin his day. He had a sense of giving up and that was something I wasn't used to and something that made me personally sad. With this being said, I cannot compare or even come close to relating to the pain he was feeling, but it just saddened me to see how he was letting it dictate his emotions so much.

Taking It Out on Family Members

Going back to his personality, the worst part about the changes in my dad's emotions and attitude was how his anger wasn't just taken out on strangers; it was taken out on all of our family. Family dinners would start great but end in an argument or fight. Holidays started great but ended in fighting. Family vacations, the first couple days great, then disagreements and disputes started. My father is naturally hardheaded and opinionated, but with the changes in who he was from the medications, he was putting in his body, these times only amplified the aggression and hostility. I have so many memories of family dinners and holidays that took a turn so quickly and went from laughs to cussing and arguing. I specifically remember one vacation where my mom, dad, brother, sister, and I went on a family vacation to Florida. To this day, it's one of the scariest, saddest, most awkward, and hostile vacations I've ever been on. I don't fully remember what prompted the issue, but one thing led to another to where my dad and brother were chest to chest yelling, cussing, and my dad saying, "Alright, big guy, why don't you fuckin' hit me, you big man." Then my mom got involved, followed by my sister, and before you knew it, everyone was arguing, yelling, and screaming. Things were said that night that I never want to repeat or relive. It was a literal nightmare, and after that, we never really bounced back on that trip. Sadly, that was one of the last family vacations we went on.

One last story I'll share happened when I tagged along as a youngster on a trip to Las Vegas with my parents and my aunt and uncle. Per usual, an argument broke out eventually. My dad just got out of our car and walked away. Then we were stuck driving around looking for him. Eventually they found him on the side of the road, but once again, emotions got the better of my dad, and, as a result, it affected his actions, which led to another dysfunctional and drama-packed trip.

For me, there were always mixed emotions when it came to family gatherings. On one side, I was so excited to be able to hang and laugh and see my family. While on the other side, I was nervous and somewhat anxious about how my dad was going to act and who would be the one to irk my dad or have something said to ignite an argument. I know I wasn't the only one who would tread lightly around my dad, and that's unfortunate that at family gatherings when everyone is supposed to be the most relaxed, we had to keep our guard up.

Then at home, during normal days, there was never really a day that went by without an argument between my mom and dad. I can't point out specific occasions, but the arguments were steady, consistent, and aggressive. It made it very uncomfortable for me as a young adolescent because I really didn't have much of a voice and, honestly, I didn't want that wrath coming my direction at all. So, like a coward, I sat there or just overheard the constant battles my mom and dad had.

My mom is so incredible and tough to handle all these arguments. She was caring and supportive when she needed to be but was also firm and wouldn't back down from my dad when he was clearly being rude. If I endured what my mom went through, I'm not sure I would still love my dad like she does. Truly, my dad was mean to my mom at times. He really verbally attacked her at times that I was in true shock that I was actually hearing what I was hearing. With this, there was a specific time when, after an argument, I went to check on my mom and had never seen her so defeated and tired. She was clearly upset, looked at me, and told me that she may need time apart from dad and just get away. She reiterated how sick and tired she was with all of it. That made so many thoughts run through my head about what our family's future would look like. I had never seen my mom so defeated; that hurt and is something I never want to see again for the rest of my life.

It really just baffled me looking back how someone could talk so poorly to someone that they loved and who genuinely loved and supported them back. From my siblings to my aunt and uncle to my mom and occasionally to me how could you so freely and effortlessly talk to your family in such a hostile way? We all knew that person wasn't our real dad, husband, or brother.

Overall, there were countless events and situations that arose because my dad was literally out of his mind. When I was writing this section, I was really thinking hard about certain events that would depict how my dad acted, but I really struggled to remember those specific occasions because it seemed like this time in all of our lives was one constant fight. All the arguments in my mind seemed to just blend together. Playing sports my whole life, there's the idea of an athlete having a short memory and moving on to the next play. For me, those are memories I don't want to associate with my dad, our relationship, or our family as a whole. So, as a result, I've taken this short-term memory approach and pushed to move on and leave those memories in the past.

Road To Recovery

Now, in those dark times, there seemed to be no light at the end of the tunnel for my dad or his actions and the effects they were having on our whole family. But something within him finally clicked where he saw the consequences of his actions and the challenges and strains, he was putting our family through. My dad found the strength inside of him to make a rehabilitation program where he would drop one tablet a month until he was clean. Through this journey, he had to deal with withdrawal, temptation, and pain. Yet, he never gave in and never gave up. It was still difficult if not more difficult to handle the pain with no crutch. There was still arguing and still fighting, but my dad was more in control and less aggressive. Slowly, I was getting my dad back and enjoying being around him.

I didn't see as much of his recovery, as I was in college, but just talking to him on the phone and hearing his support was really awesome. During the dark times, there wasn't much verbal support or encouragement that came from him. If there was criticism, it wasn't constructive, but during his recovery, his personality really changed, and, as a result, I wanted to tell him exciting news, ask for advice, or simply just talk to him. I know my dad would never intentionally try to put me down, but when he was on his medication, he wasn't thinking straight and, because of this, said things or did things as a way to express his pain he was dealing with internally. I absolutely forgive him for all that he said or did because I know it wasn't him, and, more importantly, he recognized his wrongdoing, took accountability for it, and apologized and bettered himself to make his life and our family's life enjoyable.

As my dad got better, he started to use golf as a way of therapy. I think for anyone dealing with similar issues or temptations, they should find a hobby that not only distracts them but brings happiness and discipline in their life. In a non-cheesy way, golf has been so good for my dad and continues to teach him valuable life lessons. When you're golfing and hit a bad shot, it's easy to reload and hit another shot, or you can deflect that temptation, accept the bad shot, and move on and focus on the challenge ahead. This mindset is very applicable for my dad's personal temptations. I'm sure there are days when he's in pain and would love to just pop one pill and take the easy route, but he's able to accept that pain and move on. As my dad says, "Golf is an 18-round fight" and I feel the same is applicable to life. You have to roll with the punches, embrace the challenges, and see the positives. Golf has strengthened this discipline and willingness to "fight" when you're in a tough position. Golf has also been a great way for my dad and me to reconnect. It's a sport we both genuinely love, and I can say it's one of the most exciting things I look forward to doing with him. Golf has strengthened our relationship and really brought us tighter and solidified our bond.

As I close, I can't give enough thanks to God for helping get my family and me through the ups and downs. He has heard many of my personal prayers and I know he has impacted my dad in so many ways. The Lord answered our prayers, and I cannot thank him enough for the stability, strength, and love he has bestowed on our family.

My dad has been put through the wringer and has dragged many of us with him through this journey, but he found the strength to push, to fight, and to conquer. He's living proof that even at your lowest low, there's still hope and opportunity. I'm so blessed to have my dad back and am so proud of what he has overcome. It can be done, and he's living proof that there is a way.

Brad

Bradley (Brad) has always been the kid who wanted to be outside playing sports all the time. I mean literally. If there were any kids playing out front, he was out there. He always preferred to play some sort of sport, but if that wasn't in the cards, he would join in whatever might be happening.

When Brad was around 2 years old, I was still smoking cigarettes. When it was time for me to go out to have my after-dinner cigarette, Brad was always in tow with a ball.

As I would sit on the bench by the front door enjoying my cigarette, Brad would be at the other end of the walkway. I would roll the ball, bounce the ball, and throw the ball to him well after putting my cigarette out. I quit smoking when Brad was 4 years old and have never smoked another cigarette since.

Most of Brad's school years were spent living with a father who was on opioids as "pain medication". I want to think he somewhat understood what I was going through, living every day with excruciating pain. Even if he did have some grasp of my situation, I'm sure he didn't completely get it.

Unlike Brett and Erica, Brad had no other choice but to deal with my condition. In comparison, Brett and Erica were only subjected to my addiction half of the time due to the shared custody. Not to say that they didn't have their share of pain and disappointment.

As much as I hated not having Brett and Erica living with me full time, it was kind of a benefit for me not to see the pain in their eyes continuously as I did with Brad.

As Brad grew older, I think he learned to cope with me and my condition a bit easier. With his sports, school, and other activities, his time at home became more limited.

Brad has always had a great network of friends. They remain very close to this day, seizing every opportunity to get together when time allows, considering most of them have relocated to other cities due to their careers.

When they were young and wanted to hang out after school, I know Brad had a lot of concern about heading back to our house with his friends. In the back of his mind, he had to be thinking what condition his father, the addict, would be in.

I'm not sure if Brad or any other of my family or friends ever considered me to be a drug addict, even though they knew I was taking the pain meds every day and several times a day.

Even in the worst of times, I never recall hearing anyone refer to me as a drug addict. Maybe they were just able to refrain from using that derogatory term. I just don't know for sure what they thought.

At Brad's sporting events, he had to have a lot of undue stress put upon him by me being in attendance, never knowing when I might erupt and say or do something embarrassing.

I have a deep voice, so I'm told, and that my voice carries. When I disagreed with a call an official made during one of his basketball, volleyball, or even a football game, I tended to voice my displeasure with the call loudly. Never being disparaging, but always making my case. At least, that's what I thought at the time.

No kid should have to carry the burden of not knowing when his father might make an ass of himself. Now, after 10 years of being drug-free, I feel like Brad understands a lot more about what I went through, and hopefully, he has forgiven me to a certain degree. Hopefully!

When Brad graduated from college, he decided he wanted to serve his country by enlisting in the United States Air Force and was assigned to Joint Base Charleston, South Carolina.

It wasn't long after his arrival in Charleston that he was selected for deployment to the Middle East, to Kuwait to be exact. He deployed in January of 2020 for what was supposed to be a 6-month deployment, which ended up being over 7 months. He returned home safely in late August, and about a month later, he got married.

Brad married his high school sweetheart, Maddie, who is the love of his life. Their marriage ceremony was a challenge due to the COVID pandemic.

They had a wonderful wedding planned for October 11th, 2020, at a beautiful wedding venue in SoCal. Unfortunately for them, as for thousands of other weddings across the United States, it had to be canceled due to the lockdown. Because of this, they proceeded with an intimate ceremony at the Glider port in La Jolla.

After their wedding, Maddie made the move to Mt. Pleasant, South Carolina, where they started their lives as a married couple. Mount Pleasant is located just across the river from Charleston. They've both adapted very well to married life and the Charleston lifestyle.

Love you, Brad and Maddie!

Chapter 30: My Three Dogs

Shaddy

I always had the benefit of having a dog around while I was recovering from surgery except for a couple of weeks after losing Shaddy. Shaddy's official name was Shadow, but we called him "Shaddy" or "Shaddy-boy".

Shaddy was adopted as an 8-week-old puppy by Chris from Battersea Dog's Home in London, England. He followed her everywhere, hence his name. When Chris first came to the United States on her 6-month visa, her parents volunteered to care for him. At the time, her parents lived in Stock, a small country village in Essex about 30 miles outside of London.

Chris's parents walked Shaddy every day, going down their road, into the woods and over the fields where Shaddy loved to run. He was definitely spoiled under the care of Chris's parents, with tea every afternoon, and Sunday lunches!

After Chris and I were married in 1993, we went to England to gather all her personal belongings. We prepared Shaddy for all the legalities that were required for his trip to the United States. This included a rabies shot and a stack of documents from the veterinarian. Chris's parents purchased a travel crate for him for his flight from London Heathrow to LAX in Los Angeles.

I have a quick funny story from this trip. It's one of those events when you remember exactly where you were when you heard it or saw it.

Chris and I had been out for the day visiting some of her longtime friends, and when we returned to her parent's house, Chris's mother, Pam, asked me if I knew a person named OJ Simpson.

When I said, "Yes, I know who he is," she went and turned on the TV. Pam explained that OJ had been on the TV all day and was considered a suspect in his wife's and her friend's murders.

We found a TV station that was covering his (slow) high-speed chase down the freeway, and I couldn't believe what I was seeing. I was thinking, "What an idiot!" Personally, I believe he was guilty as hell and got away with murder.

We returned to the United States with Shaddy, landing late in the night at Los Angeles International Airport. Once we landed and went through the U.S. Customs, we were required to take Shaddy along with all his documentation to a specific location for animal inspection. When we got to the inspection center, there was no one there to inspect all his paperwork. We were a little disappointed, considering the time, effort, and cost involved to meet the required protocol for Shaddy's entrance into the United States. Even though we didn't have to go through this special inspection for Shaddy, it certainly expedited our progress through the airport and began our road trip down the freeway to San Diego.

Shaddy was the first dog and fur-baby Chris and I shared together. My first back surgery was the hardest of all my surgeries to recover from, and Shaddy played a huge part in my recovery.

After the surgery, I had to exercise as much as possible to get my body back in good shape, so Shaddy and I got into the routine of walking every day. Shaddy demanded this daily walk, and he knew exactly what time of day that walk should be, which kept me religiously on track. I think he knew it was for my own good and our special time to share. He had an accurate internal clock, especially when it came to exercise or dinner!

Sadly, soon after my second surgery, we lost him. Shaddy was almost 16 years old when he passed away. He left a massive hole in our hearts. **We love you, Shaddy.**

Harley

The house was so quiet and empty without Shaddy, and Chris couldn't stand it, as he had been her baby and Brad had grown up with him. It only took a couple of months before she and Brad went out looking for a new puppy, and they ended up bringing home Harley, an adorable, medium sized Beagle who was only 8 weeks old when he joined our family. He was so small; I could hold him in the palm of my hand.

Harley was our second dog together. He was 100% Beagle and quite the howler. He would howl at sirens, the doorbell, for his dinner, pretty much anything he wanted to. His howling was never out of control, and it was just his way of talking to us. He would use different levels of howling depending on what was going on and if you were paying attention to him.

Harley used to sleep on our bed with us at night, and he would stay there with me during the day and keep an eye on me while I went through my withdrawal. He was very loyal and caring, but he wouldn't take any of my crap. The one thing about Harley was that he was extremely protective of his family, especially Chris and Brad. If there was ever an argument or I got loud or angry, he would firmly plant himself between them and me, growling and barking—his way of telling me to knock it off.

When the time came to move to Florida, Harley was suffering from some health issues, so we couldn't travel by plane, which would have put his life at risk. So instead of flying across the country, we decided to take a road trip and drive the 2,400 miles to Florida.

Harley rode in the back of Chris's Volkswagen CC. He had his own little "suite" in the back seat, where he rode secured in a hammock with a bed, blankets, pillows, and a spill-proof water bowl. Harley had never enjoyed riding in the car, and we worried about the long journey. He spent the entire first day in the car standing up and just couldn't relax. As time went on, he became a lot more comfortable and took the new routine of being in the car every day in stride. He got used to lying down and dozing during the journey, but he still couldn't figure out what the large, noisy semi-trucks were. Every time we passed a big rig, he would pop right up to see what was going on!

We planned the trip for an easy 5-day drive across the United States, taking into consideration Harley and his relief stops and Chris and her Starbuck stops. We had made reservations to stay the nights on the road at only pet-friendly hotels, and that worked out great.

It was quite a journey, so Chris and I shared the driving. We stayed in El Paso, Texas, a 750-mile drive from San Diego the first night. The second night's stay was spent in San Antonio, Texas, about a 550-mile drive from El Paso. We stopped in Baton Rouge, Louisiana, the third night, another 500-mile drive. Then the fourth and final night of the road trip, we stayed in Tallahassee, Florida, just a short drive, this time of a little over 400 miles. Our final day of driving from Tallahassee to Winter Garden, Florida, was a short 225-mile drive.

Harley successfully survived the road trip, loved his new home, and was able to enjoy the Florida lifestyle for about 2 years before he sadly passed away from a heart condition that he'd had ever since he was a puppy. He was 11 years old. **We love you, Harley.**

Charlie

After the passing of Harley, once again we only lasted a couple of months before seeking out a new fur-baby to join our family.

On several occasions, Chris and I went out looking for a puppy visiting all the local shelters and didn't have any luck until someone mentioned the South Lake Animal Rescue Adoption Center near us in Groveland, FL.

The following day we decided to drive out to the rescue center and see if there were any puppies waiting to be adopted. You know where this is going, right?

When we arrived at the adoption center and went into the reception area, there were several areas sectioned off with families spending time with a particular cat or dog to see if they were a good fit for them.

We ventured into the wire cage kennels at the back to view the many dogs that were waiting to be adopted. It was very sad walking around looking at their sad eyes. We just wanted to take them all home with us.

We approached this kennel with 2 little puppies lying down on the concrete floor watching us. Both puppies were mixed breed and appeared to have some Beagle in them, and we have a soft spot for Beagles.

We asked for some more information on these 2 little guys and were told they were brothers and the last 2 remaining to be adopted from a litter of 5. We were told they were part Beagle and part Coonhound and would probably grow to around 40-50 pounds.

Chris and I decided to choose one of the brothers, and Chris told me the choice was mine. They were very much alike, except one of them had a tiny scratch on his nose from an apparent scuffle. I kind of liked that; he also had beautiful, soulful eyes, so he was the one we chose. He had been given the name Benny at the shelter.

We filled out the application for adoption that day, on a Saturday, and were told that it could take up to 3 days to complete our background check to ensure we would be good and trustworthy fur-parents. They said they would also contact the veterinarian who had cared for Harley to make sure there was nothing out of the ordinary.

Thus, we figured we could bring our new puppy home by Tuesday or Wednesday.

The next day, Sunday, we decided to go back to the Adoption Center to look at him again, make sure we hadn't made a hurried decision, and took Chris's parents with us to visit him.

When we got there, we went straight back to see him, hang out and watch him for a while, but as we approached his kennel, he was nowhere to be seen.

Our first thought was that someone came in after us and adopted him before getting our background check completed. We were so disappointed. We rushed back to the front desk and asked about him and were told he was just outside getting a bath; what a relief!

After Benny was returned to his kennel, we spent some time playing with him. Within a few minutes, one of the assistants came up to us and said the background was completed, and we could take him home with us today if we wanted to. Oh, hell yes, we completed the final paperwork, gave our donation, and he was off to his new home.

Once we got home, we took photos of him and sent the pictures to our kids. We asked them for suggestions for a new name. The kids suggested many different names, but the winner was "Charlie."

As it turned out, Charlie grew to be around 75 pounds, not the 40-50 pounds as we had been led to believe. The joke was on us, but it didn't matter if he was 200 pounds; we loved him.

Charlie is such a wonderful member of the family, and he has all our love. He also spends a lot of time with Chris's parents, who take great care of him, especially when we're away traveling. I must say, I've never met a more laid-back, sociable, and friendly dog in my life. **We love you, Charlie.**

I've had 3 different dogs during my 3 spinal surgeries and addiction recovery, and I can say, without a doubt, that all 3 dogs were aware of my injuries and struggles. I believe they knew how much comfort they provided me during my recovery process because all of them spent time at my side, monitoring me and keeping me company.

Another blessing, they truly are "Man's Best Friend."

Chapter 31: The Guilt and the Blessing of Being Clean

I've had to apologize so many times for all the pain and anguish I subjected everyone near and dear to me to during my addiction. These apologies might be for something I did or said. I'm sure my apologies had started to fall on deaf ears due to their frequency.

I can honestly say, every time I apologized it was meant with absolute sincerity. The one thing I'll never lose is the guilt that I carry for all the times of my bad behavior. I lost a lot of things during my addiction, physically and mentally, but I never lost my conscience.

Throughout the years of being drug-free and repeatedly apologizing for my past, I have come to these conclusions: I cannot apologize anymore. I cannot bleed anymore for my past behavior. I cannot get bruised anymore by people's perceptions of me. I can't change the past. My apologies have either been accepted, or they have not. There won't be any more apologies coming from me for my past.

When I say there won't be any more apologizing, I don't mean that I've forgotten about all my evil deeds; it just means that I've put all those haunting memories into a locked dark place in my mind, hopefully never to be revisited again.

Unfortunately, this place had to be forced open so that I could write this book. It has been very difficult to relive some of those memories, but it has also reminded me just how far I've come from my days of addiction.

When I was on the drugs and looked around, my vision was a little warped. Back then, what I saw didn't have the vibrant color that everything now has; it was basically black, white, and gray.

Not that my vision was messed up, it was just the way my brain was interpreting what I was looking at, almost as if I were watching a movie of my life from the outside, like an out-of-body experience.

After 5 or 6 years of sobriety, I committed to putting all the drama from the past behind me and just move forward in the best way possible. With my new attitude toward life, I can see everything much clearer. Every color is more vibrant, nature is more beautiful, the skies are bluer, and all the lakes, rivers, and oceans sparkle more.

I am at peace with where I am at today. I've accepted my limitations in my physical strength and condition. I've accepted the pain that I'll have to endure every day for the rest of my life. I've accepted the fact that I am a "recovering addict." I've accepted the irrevocable damage and scars I inflicted on all my family and friends. I've accepted that not all my relationships will ever get completely mended to the point they were before my addiction.

That's a lot of acceptance, I must say!

One of my goals for the distribution of my book is that it will be readily available for anyone, especially people who are currently fighting the demon of addiction to some substance, including alcohol, and are seriously contemplating getting clean.

Today, I'm sure almost everyone either knows or has known someone who has had an addiction. If you can honestly say that you've never known anyone affected by addiction, I would say that you're in a tiny percentage of Americans who have never had to deal with this type of personal crisis. **Consider yourself very fortunate!**

For the people who've had to deal with an addict daily, hopefully, what you've read about the experiences my loved ones had to endure brought some clarity to you. People in this situation have a lot in common. The following are just a few examples of commonality:

• It might be the change in the addict's personality.

• It might be the fear of how the addict can angrily explode without warning.

• It might be how distant and unsociable the addict has become.

• It might be the lack of enthusiasm or interest in doing anything.

I can go on and on and on, but I think you get the drift.

One of the worst possible circumstances that can happen would be for the people surrounding the addict to turn on the blinders and ignore the crisis. By doing this, you're basically allowing the addict to continue on a destructive path that needs to be stopped, not only for themselves but for everyone else. Condoning this behavior isn't a winning solution. The addiction is never going to go away by itself, and you're naively dreaming if you think it is.

At some point, the only choice is "tough love".

You may be a loved one or just a good friend who has witnessed the deterioration of the addict's personality and physical appearance and take it upon yourself to get involved and do everything in your power to help. In my experience, you should only take up the battle of assisting the addict in getting clean when you're completely assured that the addict is 100% committed.

The addict should understand that the path to sobriety is a two-way street. The person offering their assistance will carefully monitor every moment of their life until the journey is completed. Don't blow this opportunity for aid because they may not offer their help again if you blow it. I can't emphasize it enough.

Hopefully, both the addict and their supporters have learned from or taken away something from my book that they can relate to or find helpful. I didn't follow any manual for my road to recovery. I guess I just took some of the suggestions that were offered to me and ignored others that came from people who've never had to deal with an addicted person and the collateral damage that goes with it. There will always be those people who think they know everything but actually don't know anything. Then there are also people who are always going to have an opinion when they have no idea at all.

I took some of the professional advice that was provided, along with some loved one's advice and suggestions, and kind of customized my own recipe for getting off the drugs. My recipe was perfect for me but I'm not saying it would be a perfect recipe for everyone who wants to get clean and sober.

It may be that you can build around some of the approaches I took or maybe not, or just learn from my experiences. Everybody's DNA is different, and the mind reacts to things differently for other people. Essentially, everyone should keep an open mind to all options available for help and never discount any of them. If an option isn't working or not a good fit for whatever reason, don't continue with it. It will only worsen the situation for everyone involved, and it will lessen the chances of a complete and lifelong recovery.

You don't want that to happen, for this opportunity may never come along again.

Chapter 32: My Hobbies Before and After

Growing up, I was a very active person. I played about every sport there was just like most boys.

I started to surf when I was around 10 years old and continued up until my injury. Each time I went surfing, I would write where I went and how the waves were on a calendar. I documented my surfing for many years. One of the years, I went surfing over 300 times!

There would be days when I'd go surfing in the morning and head back for another session in the evening. In general, the wind would be minimal in the mornings and evenings, making the ocean very smooth and calm for nice clean waves.

When I was younger and went surfing, there wouldn't be many surfers out there fighting for every wave. As I grew older, the surfing crowds became too much, especially with all the newbies trying to learn how to surf. The beginners were usually naive and didn't understand the proper etiquette for catching waves, which caused collisions and surfboard damage.

On several occasions, we would surf in the morning and then head up to Big Bear Mountain for an afternoon of snow skiing - a nice benefit of growing up in Southern California. I never got the opportunity to learn to snowboard. Snowboarding really didn't become popular until after my injury. I always thought snowboarding would come naturally to me, considering all the time I had spent on surfboards and skateboards growing up.

Another sport I've become passionate about is golf. Golf was one of the very few sports that, growing up, I had zero interest in learning or playing. I could never understand the excitement and fun people had for this sport until I was around 21 years old. One of my friends was getting married, and it was decided that all the boys would go play golf before the evening bachelor party. As I wanted to participate in the festivities along with everyone else, I decided to give golf a go. I had knocked the golf ball around a bit on a few different occasions, and I understood the rules and the scoring, so I wasn't completely ignorant.

We all headed to the San Carlos Golf Course located in the neighborhood that we all had grown up in. All the golf clubs were loaded onto the golf carts, along with an ice chest loaded with beer and booze. It only took playing a few holes to know this was a sport I could really get into.

I consider myself a recreational golfer and have been trying to master the game for over 40 years, off and on. The periods of off and on were due to my back surgeries and the time it took to get back to being physically able to play.

For a lot of recreational golfers, one of the goals is to not score over the century mark, a score of 100 or more. I never take a round too seriously, although I might get a little frustrated at times, but never to the point of throwing a club, which I've witnessed on more than one occasion, which looks very stupid and is immature.

I have a theory about playing golf that I like to explain like this:

A round of golf is 18 holes, so just pretend you're in an 18 round boxing match. If you get beat up and lose one of the rounds in a boxing match, that doesn't mean you've lost the whole fight. There are another 17 rounds to make it up, just like there are another 17 holes in golf to get your act together.

If you have a bad hole, get over it and move on to the next hole. Don't throw the round away just because you've had one nasty hole. Pull your pants up and grind it out. My game has improved considerably over the years, and my goal is to score in the lower 80s or even better continually.

I've had the pleasure of being able to golf with both of my sons throughout their lives. The only exceptions were during the times of my surgeries and recovery periods.

Brett, my eldest son, is a good golfer and can hit the shit out of the ball. I think, over the years, Brett has lost some interest in the game, but he drops everything at the opportunity to play with me.

My youngest son, Brad, scores consistently in the 70s or, at worst, in the very low 80s. He's a lefty and will take the challenge any hole has to offer, unlike me. I play and try to manage the course. That means I don't really take the risk-reward shots that he does! I've played a lot more golf with Brad than Brett, but that's only because there haven't been as many opportunities with everyone's busy schedules.

One of the benefits when golfing with my sons is that if they have any kind of personal issue, it will come up during a round of golf. Spending 4 or 5 hours together playing golf allows a lot of time to talk things out. I'm honored that they want to play with me. The time we spend together is priceless.

Golf has been the best therapy I could have ever had. There's something about being outside in the sunshine, taking in the views the course has to offer and watching the wildlife that use the golf course as their sanctuary. This is so true down here in Florida. There are so many lakes and ponds here that are home to all sorts of large birds, including cranes, geese, hawks, bald eagles, etc., and of course, the alligators and turtles.

Unfortunately, my golf swing isn't the prettiest because of the limited rotation of my back, which is required for a proper swing to get a good distance. I basically just have to use my upper body strength.

Watching me trying to tee up the ball on the tee box isn't a pretty sight either because of my inability to bend over, so I have to squat down like a lady, which, for a man, is a little humiliating!

In the time it takes to get home from the course, I become so stiff that I almost can't get out of the car. When I do make it out of the car, my next problem is getting my legs to start working again, but I find all the pain and stiffness are worth it, especially for my mental health. I am truly blessed to be able to go play no matter how unorthodox my game is. I can bet no one is watching and taking lessons from me! Over time, I've learned to swallow my pride and adapt to many tasks.

Oh well, at least I'm alive and not dependent on the drugs anymore.

Another thing I've lost is the ability to run. Not that I was ever a person who would run miles a day but losing that ability has been hard to accept. I can no longer be subjected to the pounding the back and spine take during running. I would be severely putting my back at risk of further damage requiring more treatment.

I'm sure most people around the age of 50 years or more have experienced some loss of their strength and ability, even if they want to admit it or not. Just remember, your physical condition could always be worse than it is, so be grateful.

Chapter 33: Comfortable Sharing My Addiction

Below is a Facebook post I posted 2 weeks after my 8th anniversary of being drug-free. Finally, being comfortable and confident I would never relapse, I decided to air my dirty laundry on Facebook for everyone to see.

The post might be a bit redundant, but my intentions are to show how much love and support I had from my family and friends during my darkest days and the love and support I continue to have from them today.

Hopefully, for the ones out there who have an addiction, the comments and feedback will help convince you that you're not alone with your addiction. You can't successfully get clean doing it alone, and people can't help you if you don't eat your pride and open-up.

The comments will also illustrate how tremendous the opioid crisis is and how it has affected so many of us in one way or another. Not only for the addict but all the collateral damage it has caused for family and friends.

Greg Neas
January 15, 2020

I want to share the path that life has taken me on. In 2001 I had an injury that required a 2 level spinal fusion. 3 years later I had to have another spinal fusion and 3 years later another spinal fusion. During my recovery I was prescribed a cocktail of narcotics (pain management) that included 8 Oxycontin and 8 Soma A DAY. Some consider this narcotic cocktail "the rich man heroin". After nearly 10 years of this "pain management" I had had enough.
With the love and support of all my family I made a decision to get off this so-called pain management. My Doctor and I came up with a rehab treatment plan. This plan consisted of me reducing just 1 tablet a month. Sounds easy, but unfortunately it was the toughest thing I have ever had to battle. The moment you reduce your intake of drugs your mind knows it's getting short changed and goes looking for the drug in every bit of your body causing excruciating pain and discomfort. It took nearly 2 years for complete withdrawal from the narcotics.
With my faith, my family, and friends I have been narcotic free for 8 years. At times it hasn't been easy. For many years after my complete withdrawal my brain often went looking for the drugs that I fed my body for 10 years, causing discomfort similar to flu. Just a little reminder that recovery is day by day.
We all know people that have or had drug or alcohol dependency. I wanted to share my story to show people that if you do have a dependency there is hope. Your mind, faith, family, and friends are all tools there to help you.
I would be happy to talk to anyone that may need assistance but don't know where to start.
The picture of my 8 year Narcotics Anonymous chip is a sign of how strong your body and mind are.

The FaceBook image includes dozens of responses to the initial post:

"Way to go keep it up."

"Damn proud of you Greg Neas. I will continue to pray for you, for peace and strength every day, and for your family and for continued support."

"Thank you for sharing, Greg. You're an unbelievably strong and loving man. A blessing to all who know you. Sending love and hugs."

"Congratulations Greg, and God Bless you my friend!

"Thanks so much for sharing your story! So many others are experiencing similar issues, and it helps to know they're not alone. Sending you my love and prayers."

"I'm really proud of you Greg. Such a wonderful accomplishment. You are very strong."

"Congratulations Greg. I know how tough it is as I am in the same fight"

Greg and friend then converse on a sub-thread to John's original comment:
"Anything I can do to help, please reach out John"

"Thank you and the same to you. Mine involved alcohol also but staying the course also. Sounds like we both started our journeys the same way. Unintentional after a traumatic injury"
"Stay strong buddy!"
"You too, stay the course"

Back to the original comments in the thread:

"Good job Greg"

"Glad you took that journey...I know it had to be a hard one. You are a great man and will always in my thoughts"

"Proud of you Uncle Greg! may I share this?"
"Yes, you sure can."

"Greg Neas, thank you for the courage to share and help others. We are glad to call you a neighbor and friend!"

"Nice work Buddy. Now if you could find some help with that slice."

"Congratulations! Well put!"

"Congratulations on your achievement! If you have continued back pain or reoccurring pain I encourage you to look into Dr. Kevin Pauza and the Discseel procedure, he has great success in treating post fusion pain without narcotics. Google his name of Discseel."

"Proud of you Greg. Sounds like you've had a long dark road. With the love & support of God, family & friends you didn't travel the road alone. God bless you on a new chapter in your life. Can I refer my daughter Andrea to your FB post? She's been on a lot of pain meds."

"Thanks for sharing your tough story, Greg. All our best to you & the family. Stay strong"

Congratulations Greg! 8 years is incredible. All love from the Anthony's!"

"Congratulations Greg, very proud of you! Was it too much golf?"
"Just a slip and fall."

"Awesome! I admire your bravery and courage and your willingness to share and help others. Keep up the hard work!"

"Congratulations on 8 years!"

"Congratulations Greg!!! The daughter of a recovery parent I can really appreciate your journey. Thank you so much for sharing. Wishing you strength and peace as you continue your journey. Much love, All the Manzano's. Miss you guys!!!"

"Proud and happy for you cousin, 8 years I'm sure seems like a life-time ago and it is because you now you have a life. Love you like a brother"

"You are a strong human being! Living with severe, chronic, spinal-pain, is a nightmare. Only those have experienced it, can understand. You are a fighter, warrior, champion. Congratulations!!!!"

"Awesome Greg! I appreciate your sharing"

"It happened to my father as well. Was the hardest thing he had to do. You were strong in mind and faith and body. Congratulations as you won the battle! Great story to share for others as pain management by drugs is easy by the doctors but what you have done is not but people need to know there are other options and support! God Bless Greg!!!"

"Good job Greg."

It was a VERY rough road, but I'm so proud of this man!"

"Christine Neas you were a very special and supportive part of his strength"

"Wow dude that's awesome!"

"Awesome Greg. Thanks for the courage to share."

“Classic!! Dig the treatment!!"

"Hey Greg, you definitely have a story to tell. Your family is so proud of you!! Love you Brother!!"

You are amazing uncle! Im so very proud of you!"

“Great job Greg and thanks for sharing. If just one person is touched by this post and it gives them the courage to take that first step, then you being vulnerable here is saving one life at a time. Great work.”

"Congratulations Greg!"

"Sounds incredibly horrible. I'm glad you had great family support and NA. Otherwise you wouldn't be around for our Taco Tuesday's"

"That's great Greg"

"Congratulations brother!"

"Wonderful story and self-discipline. Congratulations and prayers for continued sobriety."

"Wow! Congratulations."

"Strength, Courage, Family...wonderful that you can inspire others Greg!"

"Congratulations! That's wonderful!"

"Very cool post Greg. So happy to have you as a friend!"

"So very proud of you, Greg. I know how hard it has been at times for you and those close to you, but your strength, your faith, and the love and support of those around you have seen you through. Congratulations and keep it up, you are an inspiration to many."

"Awesome job Greg. Don't give up the fight."

"Proud of you buddy"

"Greg, thank you for sharing your amazing story of strength and courage. The years and miles are many since we were teams hanging out, but I couldn't be more proud to be your friend than I am today. Prayers for continued blessings!"

"Thank you for sharing this"

"Congratulations Dad. Real inspiration. Proud of you for the strength throughout this journey. Real man."

"Greg so powerful to hear your journey and continued work. Sending prayers and positive thoughts to you and your family"

"That is awesome, Greg! Thanks for sharing. Miss you guys!"

"So blessed to have you alive, healthy, and happy. You're a true testament to facing hell and coming out of it a better person. Glad you're finally sharing your story with everyone. It's going to help so many people."

"Congratulations! That was a real struggle! Glad you were a survivor!"

"Such a genuine and inspiring post. We are all so proud of the strength and commitment that you put in to weaning yourself off. There is a general lack in understanding of just how difficult it can be to deal with chronic pain, and I don't think anyone truly knows until they've been in your shoes. As a nurse I come in contact with an unfortunate amount of patience who have prescription drug dependencies. Unfortunately, in the majority of cases, they lack the love, support, and strength within themselves and in their social network, and as a result they continue to struggle with no end in sight. You are a great success and your story has the power to touch the MILLIONS of individuals who are currently struggling! We love you and are forever grateful for your perseverance"

"Congratulations Mad Dog!! Happy For you."

"Faith, family and friends – you are a very lucky man, Greg! Stay strong."

Chapter 34: A Letter from My Wife Chris

Hello!

I'm Chris, a mother, stepmother, sister, daughter, aunt, and, while juggling all of these responsibilities and working full time, I'm also a wife, Greg's wife.

A wife... married to a recovering drug addict. Never, ever thought I'd say that sentence out loud.

A wife so pissed off with the medical profession for its blatant disregard for the quality of human life that I could actually... well, you get the picture.

Were the doctors just plain ignorant on the effects of opioids back in 2001, or were they getting a nice little boost to their income by prescribing these pills in gay abandon? Either way, nobody, it seems, wants to take responsibility for the worldwide epidemic that their devil-may-care attitude has caused. There are, it seems, no takers for accountability.

To this day, I still find it hard to believe how such a small, prescribed "pain reliever" had such a significant and profound impact on not only Greg's life but my life too, and the lives of our entire family.

Looking back, I still don't know how we got through this horrific ordeal or how this way of life became the "norm," but it did. I'm also still not sure why I didn't just pack up and leave, but I didn't. The love I had for Greg and our family kept me going, plus the faith that in time this horrific situation would pass, ever the optimist! What I hadn't planned on was that this "situation" was going to last for 11 very, very long years.

Pain Management My Ass!

Back in 2001, when Greg had his first major back surgery, the latest and greatest European spinal technology had not been taught or approved here in America. The procedure being used here at that time was barbaric, and there is no other word for it. I'm pleased to say that over the following few years, the surgical technology caught up, so each subsequent surgery—Greg underwent three major back surgeries in total—got a little easier, but, unfortunately, the aftermath of his chronic pain didn't.

Because of the ongoing chronic pain, the doctors, and surgeons, whom we trusted implicitly, started Greg on what was to become a life-changing journey of "pain management," prescribing a narcotic cocktail that would allow him to lead what they deemed to be a somewhat "normal" life. What a crock of bullshit!

Information on opioids and their addictive nature wasn't readily available 20 years ago like it is today. Had we known more about these God-awful addictive pills back then, we would have told the doctors that they could stick them where the sun doesn't shine… because during the next 12 years, the sun didn't shine very much over our home.

Whenever my job allowed, I accompanied Greg to his follow-up doctor visits and then to his pain management clinic appointments, and if I didn't go with him, his dad did. During every visit, he was asked the same old questions: "How bad is your pain?" and "On a scale of 1 to 10, one being…blah, blah, blah," and of course, the pain was always hovering between 9 and 10, so instead of recommending alternative therapies it was easier for them just to prescribe more tablets, stronger doses, different narcotics to be taken and mixed with other narcotics, until Greg ended up with a concoction so lethal that, on the street, it was known as "rich man's heroin." And voila! Just like that, the addiction began. Who knew that would happen so easily? We stupidly didn't. We trusted the doctors to know what they were doing. They're the professionals, right? In hindsight, this was our first truly BIG mistake.

I vividly remember one pain management appointment where they tried to give Greg a three-month prescription for well over 1,500 tablets (No! This isn't a typo) until I threw a fit and stopped them. Who in their right mind gives an addict a three-months supply of narcotics?

The New Normal?

Subsequently, Greg couldn't work at all, and even though I had always had a job, I had never been the main breadwinner. Now the tables had rapidly turned, and I had to pick up the slack. We had three kids, groceries, bills, healthcare, and college to pay for. After spending six months stressing and applying for higher-paid jobs, I was blessed to land an amazing job as a Creative Director for a hospitality company in San Diego that paid well and had great health benefits, which allowed me to support our entire family.

My new position was accountable for building and directing an in-house creative department, so the job came with great responsibility, long hours, travel, and never-ending meetings. Don't get me wrong; I loved my job. It was both demanding and uplifting, and, ultimately, it became my salvation. It kept my mind active and me so busy that I didn't wallow in self-pity and "what ifs" with the bonus that it kept me out of the house… and out of harm's way.

Between work and looking after Greg, our kids and their activities, our dog, and dealing with Greg's very temperamental ex-wife, I was stretched very thin both physically and mentally.

Every morning before I left for work, I would make sure Greg had everything he needed. Because of the pills, he spent most of the day in his large zero-gravity chair (which I purchased for him after his first surgery in hopes of easing his pain), watching TV, or sleeping. Quite frequently, he would be so depressed that he would cry before I left the house in the morning to go to work. Now, if you have ever dropped your toddler off at daycare where they have cried and begged you not to leave, then you know how this feels, so imagine how I felt with my spouse behaving in the same way. Shocking, I know. This wonderful man, who was once my rock, had become my "other" child. It was both heart-wrenching and, sorry to say, as irritating as hell, all rolled into one.

I remember driving to work praying that Greg wouldn't do anything stupid in my absence like mix up his medications or unwittingly take too many pills and that he would be okay until I got home. In the beginning, I didn't want to leave him like that, but as time wore on, I got to the point where I learned to suppress the whole scary situation as a coping mechanism, throwing myself into work so that I didn't have time to think. That may seem like a very strange and cold thing to say, but it was basically a form of self-preservation. Out of necessity, I built a mental wall, and as time marched on, the wall just got higher and stronger.

Each day, I would call Greg during my lunch break at work to check in and see how he was doing, make sure he was okay, only to have the phone answered by a belligerent, sometimes angry stranger with a slurred voice who sounded drunk off his ass. After every call, I would hang up and wonder why on earth I had bothered to call and continue to put myself through this daily trauma.

During this time, my niece, Amber, who worked with me in my office and knew firsthand what was going on, patiently spent many work breaks sitting with me at Starbucks, listening to me drone on about my predicament with her uncle. Awful, I know. She became my sounding board and confidant, and she was my rock, helping me navigate through this extremely difficult time when I really had nobody else to talk to.

To Amber: A very BIG THANK YOU for your daily patience, understanding, willingness to listen, and humor! I am forever in your debt. Love you.

I had to travel quite often for work, which Greg greatly resented, plus I didn't feel comfortable leaving our young son in Greg's care while I was gone, so I was caught between a rock and a hard place. Greg and I started to argue and fight, one minute, he would be "normal"; the next, the medication would turn him into some absurdly angry person that I didn't know or even like very much

The saddest part of this was that he was so high on opiates that he didn't think anything was wrong or out of the ordinary. He always insisted he was "perfectly fine," which became his constant catch phrase whenever I challenged him on anything. I can assure you his anger and his subsequent actions were anything but perfectly fine. He became very short tempered, picked fights with everyone over nothing in particular, couldn't deal with thinking or doing more than one thing at a time, and was often verbally abusive to me and anyone within earshot, something I tried very hard to shield our kids from whenever possible. To this day, it still turns my stomach to realize I didn't do as great of a job of protecting them as I had thought.

Hindsight is 2020

When Greg asked me to write my recollections of this dark time in our lives, I procrastinated for many months. Mainly for these three reasons. Firstly, I didn't know where to start as all the bad things that had happened had become a tangled mess in my memory. Secondly, I didn't want to drag up all the memories that I had (successfully, I thought) buried. And thirdly, I really didn't want to make Greg feel worse than I know he already does.

But he was persistent, so I forced myself to write, and it has helped me to clarify a few things, including highlighting some instances where I should have been stronger and put my foot down, or maybe even given up and left for a while to gain a better perspective. Either way, I can't say it's been an enjoyable task.

My memories are all still fragmented because I've tried to bury them as part of a "past life," but, in hindsight, I wish I had kept a journal. However, there are still some very vivid memories of events that I shall never, ever forget and can maybe never forgive. I cannot put these memories into any semblance of chronological order because they're forever muddled to me as life back then was one long roller-coaster ride. Still, I do want to share some of them, albeit in bullet point fashion. I'm not sharing these instances to make me feel better because I never will or to shame Greg but simply to explain how this horrific medication affects and hurts the addict's family almost as much as the addict.

• Greg's continual angry outbursts quietly took their toll on me. I'm a strong person. I started my own business at 21, emigrated to the United States from England on my own and became a citizen, and have worked as a female executive in corporate America for the last 20+ years; so, I've always been great at coping with anything thrown my way, until this one particular day. I hadn't realized the damage I was doing by bottling up my emotions and silently coping. I remember being in our master bathroom upstairs getting ready for work one morning and hearing someone yell, and a downstairs door slam shut, not in anger I don't think, but the noise was so loud and unexpected that I almost jumped out of my skin, and it made me physically shake. This reaction was so violent that it made me seriously question whether I should continue this journey or if trying to keep it all together was too high a price to pay for my wellbeing and that of our family.

• Greg had become very adept at maintaining a "normal" persona (most of the time) when we were out of the house, so nobody really knew the extent of his addiction, and I, like a coward, played along. It was too draining and embarrassing to try and explain his behavior, and how we all lived on the edge in private. The entire family kept his secret. Looking back, the strange thing is, that even though we understood his new persona was due to the medication, I don't think any of us truly thought of him as an addict, even though the evidence was staring us in the face, and we, unfortunately, enabled it.

• Who would drive when we went out became one of the main arguments between Greg and me. I would argue that he shouldn't drive due to all the medication, he would angrily argue that he was "perfectly fine," so I'm ashamed to admit that I let him drive on many occasions when he shouldn't have, just to avoid a huge confrontation. I was so over the arguments.

One night, we were leaving a company Christmas party, and he insisted on driving home. I was too tired and worn out to argue (I had also had a couple of cocktails) so I let him. It was quite late at night, and we were driving home on the I-15 in San Diego when another driver cut us off. This simple, though admittedly stupid act sent Greg into a complete irrational fit of anger, and a full blown, out-of-control road rage ensued. He drove like a complete lunatic swerving in and out of traffic and chasing the offending driver at a crazy speed and as if caught in a nightmare I remember screaming for him to stop, thinking that this was it, I was going to die. I finally managed to get Greg to pull off the freeway but then his anger was instead directed at me for being such a "drama queen." To this day, this entire incident makes me feel sick to my stomach.

• I have many memories of Greg flying into a rage without warning. One such instance was on the side of a freeway in Las Vegas, NV with our VW Eurovan packed full of family including our kids and their young cousins. His explosive rage caused chaos and tears amongst the family, and I remember him just getting out of the van and leaving us all stranded there on the side of the road while he walked down the side of the freeway!

There were so many times like this with the kids where I had to step in, sometimes physically, and take the brunt of his anger just to protect them. Luckily, my stepchildren, Brett and Erica, didn't live with us full-time, which I was sad about but, in hindsight, was actually a blessing. Shielding them from the constant turmoil was a little easier because they weren't around all the time. Trying to shield Brad from the insanity that was our home life was more difficult and one night it unfortunately became crystal clear that I hadn't done a good job of that.

It was late, Brad was asleep, and we were going to bed when Greg flew into an angry rampage, about what I can't remember, back then his anger could be triggered by literally anything: a wrong look, a wrong word, him dropping something, the room being too hot or too cold, usually something totally out of my control. I had learned by now not to aggravate the situation, so I calmly walked out of our bedroom, closed the door behind me, and went downstairs to sit quietly in my office so as not to disturb Brad.

I was sitting there with tears streaming down my face when I heard the patter of small feet come into the room, and a little hand came and silently held my hand. It was Brad, and I remember saying "I'm so sorry, honey, but I don't think I can take this anymore" and this small, wise beyond his years, seven-year-old just sat there gave me a hug and told me, "Everything will be alright, Mama" and "We will get through it together." His thoughtfulness both helped and hurt me. My young son shouldn't have had to become the adult. He went on to explain that "Dad hurts so much he can't help getting angry." That was one of my lowest points and I still couldn't bring myself to tell my awesome little boy the truth that it was the damn drugs, not the pain, causing his daddy's insanity.

Unfortunately, there were so many instances of complete insanity that I hit rock bottom and told Greg that he had to get his life together or we were finished. A harsh reality check after sixteen years of marriage. To my amazement, he had a moment of complete clarity and agreed that he had to get off the drugs or he knew he would lose his entire family.

I wanted him to go into rehab because I knew I wasn't qualified to take care of him on my own while he went through withdrawal, but, again, the medical profession let us down.

Greg and I paid a visit to his pain management doctor and asked if he could be admitted into rehab. The answer we received was, "You don't need rehab; you're only taking a mix of 16 (opioid) tablets a day! I have patients who are taking 80 tablets a day." Really? I mean what the actual f**k? I was furious. To Greg's credit, he pursued his request but was told that as he wasn't really taking "that many pills," he could wean himself off them at home by "simply" dropping half, then one whole tablet per month. Really?

We decided that he had to do whatever was necessary, and he was committed to weaning himself off the tablets. Unfortunately, it soon became clear that even dropping just half of one tablet per month was going to be extremely difficult, with awful withdrawal side effects, but he persevered. Every month Greg would get sick and be confined to bed for a few days with extreme flu-like symptoms: aching, chills, shakes, as the drugs slowly left his body but continued to ping his brain looking for a fix. This apparently simple, cold-turkey home regimen took two long years and many, many tough days to complete.

I'm so very proud of Greg for having the determination and stamina to get through this excruciating period. I don't think there are many addicts out there who could have done this on their own without checking into a rehab facility.

Forgive and Try to Forget

Being a creative person, I see everything in pictures, my life appears to me as a bar chart with different colored sections that track the "segments" of my life: school, college, friends, work, kids, moving, family, etc. Unfortunately, in the center of the chart my "family" bar has a very long black section. Thankfully, it's slowly being replaced by brighter colors, but there's still a way to go until it returns to a bright sunny yellow.

This year, 2022, marks the 10th anniversary of Greg's sobriety, and his life is slowly getting back on track, although, in my heart, I don't believe he'll ever be the same either physically or mentally as he was pre-opiate. There have been too many epic changes, but we will adapt. I'm not convinced anyone can bounce back from such mental and physical destruction without some lingering battle scars.

The lives of his family are also slowly healing, but, unfortunately, none of us, myself, Brad, Brett, or Erica, or our extended family can say that it hasn't taken a toll on our relationship with Greg, even though our support and love for him remains strong. My self-preservation wall is coming down slowly brick by brick, but I'm not going to lie, it's a lengthy and strenuous process.

I cried a lot in the beginning feeling sorry for Greg, feeling sorry for myself, and struggling to protect our kids. So, the wall around me grew stronger until I stopped crying altogether. It's surprising to me how the body and soul learns to cope because, these days, even 12 years on, it takes something truly catastrophic or heart wrenching to bring me even close to tears.

Memories fade but the hurt never completely disappears, so we plough ahead, forge new and different relationships, work at creating new memories that focus on building a brighter future together and pray that the past will eventually evaporate into silence.

Things I Have Learned from This Journey

The road to recovery is long and painful… and it's not just the addict who suffers.

Suffering is shared equally, if differently, between all family members.

You must dig deep to support, understand, and forgive.

Everyone has a different way of coping.

Hang on tight to your memories and the love you felt before opiates tried to take that from you

Opiates should be banned from the universe!

Greg: I know we will continue our journey of healing, and I hope you can forgive me for speaking the devastating truth, as I've had to forgive your actions while you were addicted. I love you.

ADDICTION: is giving up everything for one thing.
RECOVERY is giving up one thing for everything.

"One day you will tell your story of how you overcame
what you went through …
and it will become someone else's survival guide."
-Brene Brown

What more can I say about Chris?

You're about to read all about my special woman. One thing is for certain: she has been the catalyst for my recovery and the rock of my salvation for over 25 years.

Her name has been mentioned so many times throughout my book. I'm sure by now, you have a pretty good idea what type of person Chris is and her character, but I'll go on and explain. It's not only what she has meant to me, but what she has meant to everyone around her. I can honestly say if it hadn't been for Chris, I would be dead.

All of my family had to suffer throughout my addiction, but Chris definitely suffered the most. She was the one who took the brunt of my anger that came from my self-pity and frustration.

Chris and I were only married for 8 years before I suffered my injury. The injury that led to numerous back surgeries and the next 10 years of opioid addiction. Then there were the next 2 years of me getting clean. Those 2 years of getting off the opioids were just as erratic as my years of addiction were, sometimes, even worse.

I don't know if I would have had the same conviction as she did if the roles had been reversed. I hope so, but I can't say for sure. I think even if you love someone with all your heart, there is a limit to how much you can take, and I definitely pushed her to her limit; I'm sure of that.

Many times, it seemed like our relationship was so toxic that it was beyond repair. On so many occasions, I would do or say something to her that would bring her to tears. Believe it or not, I still had a conscience and felt remorse when this happened, and it also made me feel like a real piece of shit. Making my wife cry for something I said or did was the lowest point of my life; there isn't a worse feeling, but I still did it repeatedly.

I would see so much disappointment in her eyes during this tumultuous time. The sparkle she once had in her eyes when she looked at me lost its glimmer and luster day by day. Even though I saw this happening, and it killed me inside, I felt hopeless in trying to recapture that sparkle again. So hopeless that there were times I thought our relationship had deteriorated to the point of no return. Quite often, I thought maybe it might be best for everyone if we just went our separate ways.

Splitting up was the last thing I wanted or needed at that point. Breaking up would have been the death of me. A break-up would have shut the door on any chance of me trying to get off the drugs. There would have been no motivation for me to help myself. Most likely, I would have continued using the drugs until I was either in jail or a mental facility or had died.

There were so many times Chris could have said, enough is enough and thrown me out of the house, but she didn't.

She could have packed her bags and left, possibly back to England, but she didn't.

She could have talked badly about me to the kids and others, but she didn't.

She could have distanced herself from me in the bedroom, but she didn't.

There were so many things she could have done to affect me negatively, but she didn't. All these are other examples of her character and devotion.

One of Chris's main goals was to shield everyone from me when I misbehaved, got angry, or said something stupid. Over the years of being with me behaving like this, it took a toll on everyone around me to the point where I'm sure they asked themselves if their relationship with me was worth it.

Chris became a pro at hiding her emotions when she would be out in public. Always putting on a strong persona and never letting her true emotions take over and let them be seen.

When the time came, and her bottled-up feelings and emotions hit their limit, she would quietly go somewhere and let them out. It might be in another room in the house, or she might say she was going out to run an errand. I knew what was up, especially when I might hear her crying in another room with the door closed. Again, this would make me hate myself even more than I already did.

Without a doubt, I know now that out of her love for me, she stayed by my side during these times.

As I said before, I think the timing of my decision to get sober was a godsend. I'll never really know, but Chris was pretty much at the end of the road with me, to the point of considering what other options she had. The decision I made to get clean when I did gave her hope and was a sign that indicated I had been thinking about it for a while. The subject was never discussed between us, and I think it was out of fear of what my reaction might be if we did.

As time went on and we started to talk about how I might address getting sober, I saw a little glimmer of hope in her eyes, something that had been missing for many years. That little glimmer in her eyes also gave me hope and motivation that maybe, with time, our relationship could be mended.

It was the motivation that I needed at that moment, and it became the driving force that led to my decision to change my ways and seek help. I realized the brightness and the sparkle she once had was something I needed to see when I looked at her, not the dullness that her eyes displayed during the past years.

Chris and everything she stood for, her love, devotion, commitment, loyalty, and her giving, was something I didn't want to risk losing. Knowing the risk only made me stronger and more determined to get clean and stay clean successfully.

We still have our moments of disagreements, as all couples do. But one thing is unique with us: we've been through the most challenging time any couple could face. The demons of addiction have no boundaries and test even the strongest relationships.

Now I want to talk about the many other qualities of Chris. As you now know, Chris is the stepmother to Brett and Erica, children from my previous marriage. She became their stepmother when Brett was 7 years old, and Erica was only 4.

As with any divorce, there's always animosity for the new person in your kid's life. It's just a natural instinct for the ex to harbor some disdain for the person who has somewhat replaced them. Chris had to deal with me and my addiction and everything that went along with that and the moments of discontent coming from my ex and her family.

At the beginning of our relationship, there were lots of these moments, but over time, they became less frequent. Now, after over 27 years of being together, things are much more amicable. That's not to say that all the not-so-friendly treatment aimed at Chris has been forgiven, but, at least, we've all moved on for the greater cause.

When Chris became pregnant with Brad, Chris was almost afraid to tell me. I remember coming home from work one day and her saying she had something to say to me. She insisted that I sit on the couch, which immediately made me concerned. Once we were seated, she looked into my eyes and said she was pregnant. Much to her surprise,

I was elated and wanted to know all the details. Do you know if it's a boy or a girl? When is he or she due? Are you okay with having a baby? Along with a list of other questions.

The moment Brad was born, it brought another reason to feel blessed. Not only did I have another boy, but Brett and Erica now had a brother.

Even though Brett and Erica are Brad's half-brother and half-sister, none of the three have ever referred to one another as a half-brother or half-sister. They've always introduced each other as my brother or my sister. That's such an awesome feeling to know they feel that way toward each other. That's something very special.

With Chris's illustrious career, she has held many positions of leadership. Her career has always been in the creative and marketing division of a company. She's been awarded numerous accolades for her projects. Some of the companies she's worked for were global, some local, some small, and some very large. She has always been the director of her department and led many creative teams.

No matter how demanding her position was, she always continued to learn and design. Even when she held a full-time job, she accepted freelance work on the side for friends and family.

Her spectrum of creativity has no limits. Her designs include websites, logos, branding, printed collateral, special events, invitations, billboards, signage, event planning, interior design, and the list goes on and on. There has never been a challenge that she didn't accept.

With Chris's creative mindset, she was always enlisted to help with any of the kids' school projects. Most of the time, the projects would win a top school award. Even with the little and limited free time that she had, she really enjoyed working with the kids.

On top of her career, the freelance work she took on, and helping with the kids' school projects, she also had to be my caregiver during most of the kids' school years. Talk about having a full plate. I never heard her complain about it once. She just accepted it and got on with it.

Chris has a saying she often uses when faced with a difficult situation, "Just pull up your big girl pants and get on with it!"

There's nobody else in the world that I would want to share my life with other than Chris. Coming from England with her different culture, we are somewhat polar opposites in our outlook. I think that's why our relationship has lasted the test of time, considering all the obstacles that we've been through, most of my making… but also with a tiny bit of hers — just joking!

I believe that some of the best qualities in a relationship are closeness, the intimacy and comfort, the honesty and dependability, and the security that's shared living life together.

Chris and I have traveled to many destinations throughout the years, domestically and internationally. Some of our accommodations haven't always been the best, at no fault of our own, and I've learned that I can go to sleep anywhere, under any condition, as long as Chris is by my side in bed. This feeling brings me so such comfort that words cannot express. It's just a great feeling to have with the person you love.

Love you, Chris!

Chapter 35: When That Time Comes

When you have an addiction to narcotics or any other substance and really want to get clean, you need to keep all your options open. Not every option will work, but you should never discount any of them.

The problem for me was every time I had to have surgery, I would work my ass off through physical therapy to get back to whatever was going to be the new normal for me. It seemed like each time I reached that point, my back would go out, and I would have to go under the knife again. That meant I would have to restart the whole process of physical therapy, along with the drugs.

After the second and third setbacks, I began to think I would never get back to some normalcy, and that was very discouraging. It felt like I was taking one step forward and two steps back. Trust me, the step forward was very hard to accomplish, but the steps backward seemed to come with ease.

Every person's DNA is different, so there isn't one cure or fix that works for everyone when it comes to getting clean and sober. Here are some of the common denominators that come to mind for anyone wanting to kick an addiction. You'll have to dig deep into your heart for success.

Commitment: obligated by your pledge to stay on course

Willingness: willing to accept the fact that you're an addict, and you need help

Determination: decided, resolute that you'll get through this and be successful

Faith: faith that God will always have your back during this challenge and you never compromise that faith

Support: support from everyone around you and knowing they'll never give up on you

Love: love for life and love for everyone in your life

Encouragement: encouragement can come from anyone or anything

Hope: hope that you'll never waiver from your commitment

Disappointment: fear of disappointment from everyone if you don't get clean after they've stuck with you during your addiction

The disappointment factor was one that was always on my mind, even though all the others were never far away.

For 10 years, everyone from my family to my friends never gave up on me. They accepted my erratic behavior, even though they couldn't begin to understand what triggered me to do or say things that weren't appropriate. They stood by me and even tried to excuse some of my bad behavior occasionally.

If I didn't successfully get off the drugs permanently, I knew I was jeopardizing my relationships with everyone. Failing and disappointing everyone wasn't an option. They all stood by me once but standing by me again was too much for me to ask or beg of them.

After completely getting off the drugs, I sensed many questions, concerns, and doubts about my commitment and my determination to fight in the back of everyone's mind.

"Can he win this daily fight of staying clean of narcotics?"

"Will he try to justify taking a pill just once in a while?"

"Can we trust him to be true to his promise of never having another narcotic?"

"Will he relapse?"

"Will he ever return to be the person he once was?"

I'm sure there were also many other thoughts during this challenging time. As the years have gone by since my sobriety, I feel good thinking that a lot of their concerns and doubts have been answered.

Even now, sometimes, when I'm with family and catch them looking at me, I wonder what they're thinking. Hopefully, their thoughts are only good ones now, maybe like these…

"Wow, he's made it; he's never going back to the drugs."

"I didn't realize how mentally strong he was."

"Yeah, no more phone calls about how he's messed up again."

"I'm sure glad we stood by him and didn't give up."

There was never a time when I was confronted with an intervention. That's not to say it wasn't being discussed secretly among my family.

I can honestly say that I'm quite proud of myself, accomplishing what I believe to be one of the greatest mental and physical challenges anyone can face in their lifetime. It was only achieved with the love and support of everyone around me, and I can't emphasize that enough.

If you are an addict and don't have the love and support that I had, have already lost that love and support, or never had it, there are still lots of resources out there. For example, Narcotics Anonymous and Substance Abuse and Mental Health Services Administration (SAMHSA), to name a couple.

That's why it is so crucial to accept the challenge of becoming drug-free when you still have that love and support. To try and take this challenge after everyone around you has given up on you would significantly reduce your chances for a truly successful exodus of drug use.

For those out there who are addicted to any substance and are wanting to get clean, please don't wait till you've lost everything.

Chapter 36: Never Take Life for Granted

I want to share something I witnessed recently that shows just how precious life is and how life can be taken away from you in an instant.

This was an event that many of us have thought about and, fortunately, few of us have had to experience.

I had been drug-free for almost 9 years when this happened. Witnessing this tragic event convinced me even further that I had done the right thing getting clean. I didn't want to give up on life and die. Death would have ultimately been the outcome for me if I had continued with the narcotics.

I was getting gas at Costco in Orlando one morning, and, as usual, it was very busy. Shortly after starting the gas pump, I heard a gunshot! When I looked in the direction it came from, and I saw a man running away from the Navy Federal Credit Union no more than 50 yards away from me.

Seconds later, more gunshots rang out, and everyone started to panic. People were running from the Credit Union through the gas station area, and the Costco customers were running away, leaving their cars while still pumping gas.

As people ran past me, a young girl on the other side of my pump looked at me in fear and was crying. I went right over to her, and we both knelt down behind her car. I told her, "It's okay; we're going to be fine." Roughly a dozen shots in total were fired, and after a few seconds, which felt like minutes, the gunshots stopped. That's when I told her, "Now is our chance to get out of here." We both jumped in our cars and left to get safely away.

What I thought was a robbery at the Credit Union was actually a murder. Some piece of shit thought it was acceptable to kill his wife as she entered her place of employment.

The point I'm trying to make is this: times are tough for everyone right now, and some people are very desperate. Please always be careful and vigilant, and if you see, hear, or know of anything that's not right, speak up!

Chapter 37: My Life Now

As I come to the end of my story, I would like to update you on my current status after 10 years of being sober from my addiction to opiates.

I can honestly say that it hasn't been easy. There have been several times during the past 10 years, especially after other surgeries, when I could have taken the easy road and jumped back on the opioid wagon to relieve the pain, but I didn't. At those times, I reflected on how it was when I was under the influence. These brief moments of reflection made certain that I never wanted to have another narcotic for the rest of my life.

The worst thing that could ever happen is to have a relapse! Sometimes, my pain is so acute that I must spend a day or two just lying flat in bed. This is something I'm not proud of and still hits my dignity. I understand this is what I must do in order for me to have some normalcy and get my back to reset.

I sure feel guilty about being lazy when I need to just kick it for a couple of days, but I think Chris and my family understand my need for this.

There's no one reason that brings my pain to the level that requires me to take a day or two off and rest. It might be from physically overdoing something such as yard work, and that's something I have a lot of with my current house.

It's just the fact that my back, at some point, has had just too much, and it needs a little break to return to my normal level of pain. I always try to do more physically than I probably should. For some reason, I feel like I always have to prove my worthiness to everyone, especially Chris. She's constantly voicing her concerns when I go out and do something physically demanding, reminding me how sore I'm going to be when I get done. It's something I must do, at least for my own sanity. It's also to prove to myself that I'm not a useless piece of humanity and that I still have some manhood left.

I know this sounds like a bunch of gobbledygook, but unless you have walked in my shoes, you cannot fully understand how little things like this affect a person's mentality.

While this book has taken me almost 6 months to write, it has been an emotional roller-coaster. It was rehashing all the years of pain, disappointments, embarrassment, ridicule, displeasure, and failures that my addiction has brought to me and everyone around me. It has definitely taken a toll on me.

Although most of the rehashing has been negative and hard-hitting, some of it has been rewarding for me. It has allowed me to realize I occasionally made some good choices.

When my thoughts turn negative, I think about how something went wrong and how I could have handled something differently to have a better outcome. It's also made me think just how important it is to give the decision or choice you've made some thought before having a knee-jerk reaction.

On those rare occasions when I did make the right decisions, I reflect on how that right decision made me feel good about myself and that I hadn't completely lost my mind.

Everyone who knew me throughout my years of addiction was aware of my back injury and the surgeries that followed. They understood I now had physical limitations, and they were also pretty much aware of the pain that I was going through.

They could tell by the way that I had to walk, climb a flight of stairs, bend to pick something up, or carry something. It was evident I had physical limitations, and, again, I felt the loss of pride as a man. Not that anyone ever called me out. It was just something that affected me mentally. I've gotten over that now and accepted my restrictions. It is what it is, and move on.

Although everyone had an idea about my back and my pain, I don't think many were aware of my opioid addiction. In the 10 years of my drug use, it was never brought to my attention that anyone thought of my doctor-prescribed medication as an addiction. If they did, it was never talked about with me. I never had any of my friends or acquaintances stop talking to me or stop wanting to be around me because they found out about my addiction.

Thus, I think my addiction was my and my family's "dirty little secret."

It's pretty amazing how an addict can cover their tracks and act as civilized and normal when pushed to do so, if they haven't already walked the entire length of the plank to the point where they've lost the physical appearance of a normal person. Most of us know what a full-blown junkie looks like or have at least seen one on TV.

It's difficult for an addict to go undetected, especially when it comes to the people who knew them prior to the addiction. For the people who knew the kind of person they were before, the slow deterioration of their appearance can hurt and make them feel helpless. Maybe reading my book can provide some intel on how to recognize, cope with, support, and possibly help them understand and make sense of what addiction is.

"Addiction is a disease and should be treated as one. Addiction involves changes in the functioning of the brain and body due to the continuous use of drugs, alcohol, as well as others. Over time, addiction becomes more severe, disabling, and even life-threatening. A person's DNA account for about half of the chances a person will develop an addiction." —*www.samhsa.gov*

Chris has always said that I have an addictive nature. That was even before I became an addict. She witnessed this trait of mine with other things but nothing as severe as my addiction to opioids. When I like something, I tend to over-indulge!

Even though I have the scars of my addiction, I think I've become a better person for it. I've taken advantage of my successful withdrawal from opioids to learn from my mistakes, better understand people and the challenges they face, what's important and what isn't, and accept people for who they are.

As I wrote this book, I tried to speak from my heart. I know it sounds a bit corny, but it's the truth.

When I sat down each day to continue writing my book, rarely did I ever get writer's block. Sometimes, it took a moment to get started, but when I started, the words and my thoughts would just flow.

I found it quite easy to put my thoughts into words as I wrote. My story isn't one that had to be fabricated; it just had to be relived. Writing about something as horrible as my addiction was something I really wanted to share.

I know there are a lot of books out there already about addiction, specifically about the opioid crisis. Most of these books are written by someone well known, maybe an actor, music performer, athlete, or someone else with notoriety.

I wanted to put my book out there coming from an average guy with absolutely no notoriety. Someone from the real world. Someone who didn't have the resources that people with fame do to take the fight of soberness on. The people of fame always seem to have the financial stability to seek out only the best and professional treatment available.

For me, I didn't have that option and, most likely, never will. I think this is the case for the other 99% of the addicts out there seeking help.

When we, the average persons, are confronted with the dilemma to get clean, I believe we have a stronger commitment and acceptance for the battle to get clean. As our resources are very limited, we don't have the luxury of failing and getting another chance, unlike the celebrities with unlimited resources.

When a celebrity fails, they can always have another attempt to get clean. I personally think having an option for multiple attempts makes them more vulnerable for relapse. Whereas for the common folk, we must commit and stay steadfast in our journey to abstain from our addiction.

I want to give thanks to all my friends and family who stood by me through my addiction, the 2 years it took for me to get entirely off the opioids, and the 10 years of being clean.

I've shared what my immediate family has meant to me through all of this, but I wanted to mention some of my lifelong friends who were also with me for the 20-year road trip I was on.

Mike:

I've known Mike all my life. He grew up down the street from me, and we've been the best of friends ever since first grade. We were surfing buds, camping buds, party buds, baseball buds, just the best of buds.

Through thick and thin, we've pretty much been in contact with each other for nearly 55 years. There was a period of probably 10 of those years when we were disconnected.

I think it was the fact that he wasn't living nearby anymore, and we were both busy raising our kids. When you're raising kids, your schedule starts getting dictated by their schedule, and it doesn't leave much time to get together, especially when there's some physical distance between you.

After the kids were grown, we reconnected and have been hanging out playing golf at every opportunity we get. He's even made a few trips to Florida to visit me. **Thank you, Mike!**

Steve:

I met Steve and his family around 1995 when they moved into the neighborhood directly across the street from us. The moment we met, we became friends.

He worked for Volkswagen of America and introduced me to the Volkswagen brand. I had never owned a Volkswagen up to that point, but for the next 25 years plus, that's all we've ever owned.

Steve has his own addiction, and that would be his work. He is the epitome of a "workaholic." We've enjoyed many great times together, and he is always ready to have a good time whenever his work permits.

Of all my friends, Steve probably has the best understanding of my addiction and what came along with it. All the bad with some good. **Thank you, Steve!**

Julia:

I must also give a shout-out to our house cleaner for many years, Julia. An older immigrant lady from Mexico who had a heart of gold, she cleaned our house every 2 weeks right up until we made the move to Florida. Around the Christmas holidays, she would always bring us a huge pot of homemade pork and chicken tamales, which were delicious.

When I was recovering from my surgeries or just wasn't feeling good, which was most of the time, she knew it. She would gingerly clean the house around me. She would also check in on me throughout the day to see if there was anything I needed. When she was finished, and it was time for her to leave, she would always come to me and ask one more time if I needed anything before she left. **Bless you, Julia!**

Most of my acquaintances were aware that I suffered daily with pain. Family and friends who knew me more personally understood I was taking some form of medication to help control the pain. There were only a few who knew that I had become addicted to opioids.

I've been blessed to have many friendships that have lasted ever since childhood. I also have many other friends where our friendship has lasted over 25 years or more, catching up with each other at every opportunity.

San Carlos:

I grew up in a new housing community known as San Carlos. As everyone was new, the community grew to be very close. All the kids got to know each other, as did the parents. What a great thing, and I'm so glad I got to grow up like that. That's where many of my friendships started and continue to this day.

The community of San Carlos has had its fair share of tragedies, but we've also had our share of accomplishments. As a whole, I think most of us feel the same way about how blessed we were to grow up together and wouldn't change our childhood even if they could.
Thank you, San Carlos!

It wasn't my intent for this book to be a "Doom and Gloom" story. I wanted to provide an insight into my journey that life has taken me on and how your life can change forever in a split second.

When those life-changing events happen, you have to adapt. You can either drown in your self-pity or self-destruction, or you can pull your pants up and take on the fight.

I know, pulling up your pants and taking on that fight can be easier said than done. Trust me, I definitely had my share of self-pity and loathing, but I never let it take total control of my life and my future. Once you're consumed with these feelings, it can make the task of getting clean even harder, even to the point of giving up and succumbing to the addiction.

Sometimes, during these periods of feeling sorry for myself, I believe someone was testing me, my determination, and my will to survive. I think we all know who that person was.

Now I feel confident that I'll never choose to go down the road of addiction again since I know how that road ends up. It's basically a one-way road to the gates of hell.

As we grow older, almost everyone will suffer from some sort of ailment, disease, mental, or physical disorder that will affect the way they live, no matter how big or small. When that happens, decisions have to be made in order to adapt to these new restrictions.

The best advice I can give is to accept these changes with an open mind.

• Don't give up because of a setback.

• Find the best option to manage your condition.

• Don't set overreaching goals; keep it real.

• What works for someone else may not work for you.

• Come to terms and accept whatever the case may be.

Although it can be difficult at times, try to keep your negativity limited and to yourself. The people around will eventually get tired of hearing you complain, and your relationship will suffer.

Hopefully, you now have a better understanding of the disease of addiction and what the addict has to deal with. Every moment of their life is consumed with the demons that go along with addiction.

I sincerely hope that you've enjoyed reading about the last 20 years of my life's journey. Although most of it, some will feel, has been a bit of a downer. Hopefully, there are some bits and pieces that can be inspirational to others.

Live every day like it's your last. God Bless!

When life gives you a basket of lemons, such as an injury or illness that changes the person you once were, when it restricts your ability to do what you once did, when it makes you seriously think about your worthiness as a productive human being, you just make lemonade … or go out and write a book!

Chapter 38: Hope for My Book

In writing this book, I wanted to share how your life can be changed in a second, how you must deal with the changes, and how you must be strong to face this challenge.

I don't understand why I survived my addiction, but I'm sure it will become apparent at some point. For now, I think maybe my survival allowed me the opportunity to share my story with you.

I believe wholeheartedly that my book will help educate and enlighten you about the destruction caused by opiates and give hope to other addicts and their supporters.

I want to let people know that addiction isn't a life sentence, even if it sometimes seems like it. There's light at the end of the tunnel, and that light will get even brighter as the journey to get clean becomes a reality.

There were definitely times when I wanted to give up, throw it all away, and just succumb to a life of narcotics, knowing all the time that my life on earth was no guarantee.

When these moments of despair came, I always thought about the strength of my mother, and what the harm and damage would be for my loved ones if I no longer existed.

At times, I thought all my family would be better off if I were no longer alive, but now I know I was completely wrong in thinking that.

In this book, I've tried to show the ups and downs, the trials and tribulations, and the pain and suffering that goes with being an addict or even associated with an addict.

I've also tried to go into detail about some of the choices and decisions I made that allowed me to return from drug dependency and rebuild most of my previous relationships. Notice I said, "most of them."

With certainty, I can say that relationships with all my loved ones have returned to where they were before my injury, and, in some cases, are even better. I think my 10 years of being clean have provided a lot of confidence for my family. My determination to get clean and stay clean without compromise to that commitment has carried a lot of weight and allowed me to be a part of their lives again.

For those out there experiencing a situation like mine or who know someone who is suffering from addiction, I hope this book has provided some insight and information. I wanted to help educate anyone who might be associated with an addict, whether a family member or a friend, because being in this position can be very challenging at times, especially when it comes to confrontation.

Dealing with an addict means there will definitely be times of confrontation. To the best of your ability, it's important that you understand the dire situation the addict is experiencing, not to the point of condoning their addiction or erratic behavior, but to be there for support, love, and consultation.

In my case, sometimes "tough love" had to be hammered home to me, and other times, it was a look of disappointment that got the message through to me. At the lowest and most harrowing time of my addiction, I quite often didn't care what people had to say to me, or what the expression on their faces was trying to convey to me. When I reached the point where I had lost most of my pride and self-esteem, I didn't really give a shit about anyone's feelings.

I think sometimes the addict's logic is, "If I'm miserable, everyone around me should be miserable too." Demented, I know, but it didn't matter.

You've read about my loved one's experiences with me during my addiction. How my addiction had affected their lives and even the resentment some of them had for me at the time, how they dealt with it then, and how it is now.

In some of their stories, such as my kids', I learned for the first time the resentment they had for me at that time. That was a tough pill to swallow; even though I kind of knew it in my heart, I didn't want to accept it. For their willingness and commitment to stand by me for the many years of addiction, even though I'm sure it was extremely difficult at times, the reward for us all has been worth it.

I know for a fact that if any of my family members become aware of someone currently in the situation that they found themselves in with me, they'll be the first to help by sharing what they went through, and hopefully, that will be of benefit. Either way, I know my addiction has provided them with knowledge about the risks associated with substance abuse, no matter what the substance is, how it can destroy the fabric of a person's life and that of the people around them. It has also scared them to death just how easily and quickly a person can become addicted.

If you're currently an addict, no matter the substance, I hope this book will encourage you to see that there's always a chance for recovery. The road to getting clean will be very slow and filled with obstacles, but the road is passable.

Quitting your addiction will be the toughest challenge you'll ever have to overcome. It will be a day-to-day fight for the remainder of your life. However, the struggle becomes easier as the days, weeks, months, and years go by.

Unfortunately for me, my addiction was due to my injury and the chronic pain associated with it. Because of the never-ending pain that I experience every day and will have for the rest of my life, I have a constant reminder of my past.

I've learned just how strong and powerful my mind actually is throughout these last few years. Somehow, I've taught my mind to mentally block most of my daily pain and to overcome thoughts about taking any form of opioid ever again. I'm still not sure how, but I've learned to tolerate it.

Every addict must dig deep within themselves and give a thousand percent to make the commitment to get clean. When the time comes, and you realize there's a chance to get sober, for whatever reason, grab the opportunity and mentally accept it.

This might be your one and only chance in a lifetime, so don't let it pass you by. Just remember, the continued use of drugs will only make your life more of a living hell for you and for all those around you.

Please don't wait until you have lost everything meaningful in your life to make the decision. If you have nothing to fight for, your strength, enthusiasm, and motivation to get clean and sober will be lost. When you've lost everything, there's no trophy at the finish line.

DON'T BLOW IT!

I have to credit some of my success of getting off the drugs and staying off them to my battle with nicotine. As I mentioned, I was a cigarette smoker for 20 years up until July 1999 and then made the decision to quit. Quitting smoking was one of the toughest addictions to take on, but I successfully ended it and remain a nonsmoker.

The sooner you can face your demons, the better off you're going to be, and you'll be able to begin rebuilding your life and your relationships wherever possible.

For those addicts who have traveled the road of addiction for so long to the point of losing everything, there is still hope. As the opioid crisis has exploded throughout the United States, more attention has been brought forward for the need to address the crisis. The resources for seeking help are now thankfully plentiful, and many can be found on the internet.

Even though it took 2 years to get completely clean, I was blessed with Dr. Douglas's plan for me to decrease my opioid intake. I never had the need to attend a group or individual therapy session, check into a rehabilitation facility, or even require intervention, so it worked perfectly for me. I'm not saying this plan will work for everybody, so understand that group or individual therapy, rehabilitation facilities, and sponsors are all resources available for you if you want help with your disease of addiction.

If you suffer from an addiction and want to make the leap to getting off drugs, hopefully, some of the information I've shared will be helpful. I believe getting in touch with either a physician or counselor who has been professionally trained in the field of addiction and recovery is the best start.

Ideally, with a professional's suggestion and your input, you'll come up with a plan leading to a complete and successful recovery, possibly using some of my tools as a starter or even a stepping-stone to build from, leading to a new life without drugs.

Ever since I reached the milestone of 5 years of being clean, I made the decision to offer my assistance and talk with anyone in need of help. It might be, "Where do I start?", "I'm so desperate, I'm to the point of giving up on life," or anything in between. Whatever it is, it would be my honor and pleasure to assist you at any time. Since I've been blessed with a redo for my life and considering how lucky I am to be where I'm now, I feel it's my duty to offer such help. Please reach out to me at *PerfectlyFine2022@gmail.com*

Now that I have 10 years under my belt, I feel like I've earned the right to wear some well-deserved stripes on my sleeve and have the knowledge and experience to speak about addiction. Again, I'm willing to speak to any group or individual about my past, how I got to where I am, and all the time in between.

My addiction is a scar that will be with me for the rest of my life, but it's a constant reminder of how strong and determined I can be and just how blessed I am.

THE END

My Withdrawal Journal

January 1, 2010:

I went from 8 to 7 tablets a day by eliminating one Soma. I didn't really notice a big change because I only had to cut one tablet. I now took 1 Soma in the morning, 2 at noon, 2 in the afternoon and 2 at bedtime.

February 1, 2010:

Dropped another Soma, going from 7 to 6 tablets a day. My plan was to take 1 Soma in the morning, 1 at noon, 2 in the afternoon, and 2 at bedtime totaling 6 Soma for the day. My body started to actually realize it isn't getting the normal amount.

March 1st, 2010:

One more Soma off the diet going from 6 to 5 Soma a day. 1 in the morning, 1 at noon, 1 in the afternoon, and kept taking the 2 at bedtime so I could get somewhat relaxed in order to get some sleep

April 1st, 2010:

At this point I took half the Soma I did originally. Another Soma off the menu going now from 5 to 4 a day. Seemed to be the easiest adjustment to this point for me. I was still able to take 1 Soma in the morning, 1 at noon, 1 in the afternoon, and then 1 at bedtime.

May 1st, 2010:

Now, I was at the point where I had to eliminate the Soma altogether in one of my daily doses, 4 to 3. My choice was to skip my morning Soma. I made it without a Soma till my noontime dose, and then I took 1 in the afternoon and 1 at bedtime. It was a good start, but it was also becoming more challenging mentally.

June 1st, 2010:

My daily dose of Soma has now dropped from 3 to 2. Decision time for me, which of the other dose do I eliminate completely? My decision was to take one at noon and 1 at bedtime.

July 1st, 2010:

Wow, now I only took 1 Soma for the whole day. I decided to try and wait throughout the day until I absolutely couldn't take the pain of withdrawal anymore. Most of the time I took my only Soma in my afternoon/evening dose. Occasionally I was fortunate enough to hold off until bedtime. Proud of myself, but definitely feeling the effect of the missing Soma.

August 1st, 2010:

This was the first month without any Soma and where I started a 3-month break before I began the battle of weaning of the oxycontin.

November 1st, 2010:

Now that I had cut half of an Oxy daily, going from 8 to 7 ½, I started the day by taking 1 ½ Oxy in the morning, 2 at noontime, 2 in the afternoon/evening, and then the final 2 at bedtime.

December 1st, 2010:

Time to cut out another ½ of an Oxy, going from 7 ½ down to 7 daily. My schedule was to start the day off with 1 ½ Oxy in the morning, 2 at noon, 1 ½ for the afternoon dosage, and then 2 Oxy at bedtime. By the end of December, I had removed 1 whole Oxy from my daily routine and my health was starting to go south, both mentally and physically.

January 1st, 2011:

It was now time to eliminate another ½ of an Oxy going from 7 down to 6 1/2. The question again was when I should drop that ½ throughout the day, and so I decided to eliminate it at the noontime dose.

For the month of January, I took 1 ½ Oxy in the morning, 1 ½ at noon, 1 ½ in the afternoon, and then took 2 Oxy at bedtime.

By this time, I was really feeling the withdrawal symptoms. I started feeling as if I had the flu with fever, body aches, and pain on top of the already existing daily pain I had from my injury and surgeries. Yuk!

February 1st, 2011:

This was now my fourth month of struggling to kick the Oxy addiction and the necessity to cut out another ½ of Oxy out of my routine. The math was pretty easy for me to figure out my daily dosage plan. I was down to 6 Oxy a day and the fact I was taking 4 doses a day equated to taking 1 ½ tablets each in the morning, noon, afternoon, and at bedtime. Every day my withdrawal symptoms got worse and worse and really affected my daily activities. I lost motivation and energy to do anything and became irritable while feeling like I had the never-ending flu.

March 1st, 2011:

Time again to get rid of another half, limiting my intake from 6 to just 5 ½ Oxy a day. Doing the math on this one took some thought. I had to limit one of my doses to only 1 whole tablet, but which dose would that be. My thought was that I already felt like shit when I woke up, so let it be the morning dose that took the hit. My new schedule was 1 Oxy in the morning, 1 ½ at noon, 1 ½ in the afternoon, and then 1½ at bedtime. The withdrawal symptoms were becoming unbearable and had pretty much kept me down for most of the day as I experienced gut wrenching pain and discomfort.

April 1st, 2011:

Ouch, where do I cut this month's half from? I needed to go from 5 ½ Oxy to 5 a day. With so much discomfort at this point I didn't think it really mattered. I decided to take 1 Oxy in the morning, 1 at noon, 1 ½ in the afternoon, and 1 ½ at bedtime. This is when I pretty much just laid down all day and tried to survive the day without going crazy. I didn't want to talk anybody or be around anybody at that point. I didn't want people to see the person I had become. I was depressed and started to have thoughts about my survival.

May 1st, 2011:

Now limited from 5 to only 4 ½ Oxy a day, I really started to lose my mind with the effects from withdrawal. I got up in the morning, and took 1 Oxy, and then when it was time for my noon dose, I took another 1 Oxy. I also attempted to limit my afternoon to 1, which allowed me to take the final 1 ½ at bedtime. Sometimes this pattern worked and other times it definitely did not. I felt like I was slowly disintegrating as a real-life person. I saw the changes in my physical appearance. When I looked at myself in the mirror, I would ask myself, who is this person I'm looking at? This person who is as pale as a ghost along with the deep dark eyes.

Seriously, I didn't recognize myself or didn't want to admit this is how I looked.

June 1st, 2011:

My new daily limit is down from 4 ½ Oxy to 4 a day, the math was simple. Take 1 Oxy in the morning, I at noon, 1 in the afternoon, and the final one at bedtime. I think not having to make a decision on which one of these doses I took away the ½ Oxy from, made it a bit easier to deal with. This adjustment was easy for me to figure out, but the agony of the withdrawal was becoming more and more intense, and I was suffering from it.

All the withdrawal symptoms I experienced, were like the ones I remember watching on old TV shows and movies in the past, where one of the characters was a heroin addict attempting to get off the horse (heroin). The junkie experienced chills, had the sweats, became delirious and confused... and craved orange juice!

At that time, my appetite was diminishing along with my ability to taste. The only thing I really craved most of the time was orange juice. I eventually drank OJ by the gallons, and never understood why this was.

At this point, I had successfully completed three quarters of my withdrawal process. I had completely eliminated the Soma and had eliminated half of my daily Oxy intake going from 8 Oxy to 4 a day.

I knew that I was in the fight for my life. It was only going to get harder, and I began to question if I had the strength and determination to get through this completely. I began to think about my future and what it would take to stay drug free. That's if I ultimately survived the withdrawal mentally and physically.

July 1st, 2011:

Now the fun had begun. I had to go from 4 to 3 ½ Oxy a day. How was this going to work out? My game plan was to make my morning dose only ½ of an Oxy. This allowed me to take 1 whole Oxy for the remaining 3 doses, noon, afternoon, and bedtime.

As the month went on, every morning was getting harder and harder to get through until my noon dose. By the time it came for my 1 whole Oxy at noon, I was pretty much sick and bedridden, trying with everything I had to deal with the withdrawal.

August 1st, 2011:

Okay, I stuck with the plan but barely got through July. When I woke up, I felt blessed just to be alive, but would immediately start feeling withdrawal symptoms.

Since my intake was just 1 whole Oxy, 3 times a day, the biggest challenge I faced was "How am I going to make it till my noon dose without a morning hit?" Since I was barely surviving the morning without a hit, I made a new strategy to reschedule the time that I took my doses. The plan was to try to survive without a hit until 10:00 am and then take 1 whole Oxy, then another hit at 4:00 pm, and then my last and final hit for the day at bedtime.

My body and mind had become numb, almost a lifeless feeling. When I drank the ice-cold orange juice, it was such a great sensation. Almost like I felt the cold fluid in my veins going throughout my body, making me feel alive and the numbness was gone. This feeling was short lived, making me crave more of the orange juice throughout the day, so I could experience that cool feeling again through my body.

September 1st, 2011:

2 ½ Oxy a day. What! I don't think so.

At this point I didn't think it really mattered that I was only trying to cut another ½ Oxy a day. I felt like I was out of my body looking in on myself, like a movie. Each day, I forced myself to get out of bed. I took a shower and shaved to make myself somewhat presentable. The one thing I never gave up on was my personal hygiene. I still had some pride.

My routine was to take a whole hit around 10:00am, a ½ of a hit in the afternoon or evening, and then a whole hit at bedtime. The withdrawal effects were so terrible that I really didn't notice my chronic back pain.

Just a little footnote, we had a TV/media room, and this was the room where I went every day after I got up to spend the remainder of the day trying to survive.

Chris bought me a powered zero-gravity reclining chair which allowed me to recline to the point where there was no pressure on my spine. I pretty much wore out the couch and put a lot of hours on the recliner during my withdrawal period, especially in the last year of getting clean

October 1st, 2011:

I started to see the light at the end of the tunnel and now only had the benefit of 2 Oxy a day.

My strategy was ½ hit at 10:00am, 1 whole hit in the afternoon/evening, and then the other ½ at bedtime. I referred to it as my "afternoon/evening" dose because I would wait as long as I could before taking that hit. Sometimes it would be in the afternoon and sometimes I could delay taking it until the early evening if I was lucky.

The withdrawals weren't going away, but I didn't notice them getting any worse even if they were. Had I hit rock bottom? I had the same old symptoms, but for some reason I was able to deal with them better. I still laid around, sleeping as much as possible, sometimes ending up in the fetal position by the end of the day. I think my desire to sleep as much as I could, was so I could somewhat escape, and not have to deal with the withdrawal bullshit.

November 1st, 2011:

On top of my intense withdrawal symptoms, I began to feel anxious knowing I was approaching the end of my 10 years of opiate dependency and started to feel like I might actually win this battle.

I began to get some uplifting thoughts about my future. I think my loved were also starting to feel more confident that I was going to win. None of them ever said anything about my progress or how they thought I was doing. I think they were just hanging back, keeping their fingers crossed, and hope that I would complete this train ride to sobriety

With my restricted menu of only 1 ½ Oxy a day, there was only one option for me to proceed. That option was ½ a hit sometime in the morning, ½ a hit again sometime in the afternoon/evening, and the finally a ½ at bedtime.

December 1st, 2011:

By making December 31st my last day, it meant a new start to a New Year. I had come too far and had put my family, friends, and myself through so much pain and destruction during my years of addiction on the "rich man's heroin," to fail. Some of the questions I asked myself were, can I survive on just one Oxy a day? Should I take the whole Oxy at once? Should I split the Oxy into 2 halves allowing me to take a half twice, throughout the day? When should I take these halves? The answers to all the above questions were, just man up, and take the whole hit at some point during the day. As it turned out, I found myself generally taking the hit sometime in the late afternoon.

Disclaimer Page

I am going to reference all my doctors using fictitious names to protect them and myself from any legal ramifications. I have tried to recreate events, locales, and conversations from my memories of them. Some names and identifying details of people described in this book have been altered to protect their privacy.

This book is not intended as a substitute for the medical advice of a physician.

Resources

Throughout my book I have used references from many resources. Some, but not all of them, are listed below. Some of my references are from several resources. I used certain items from separate sources and put them together based upon my personal experience. There are statements in the book that are also just my opinion. With all that I went through during the time of addiction and withdrawal, I think I have earned the right to have an opinion.

WebMD	Wikipedia
Cleveland Clinic	Healthline.com
Google	National Institute of Health
Center for Disease Control	Government Drug Information
DailyMed	MedlinePlus
Mayo Clinic	Health.gov
informedhealth.org	eMedicineHealth
Health Central	Greg's School of Survival